What Is Subjectivity?

What Is Subjectivity?

BY

JEAN-PAUL SARTRE

Translated by David Broder and Trista Selous
Introduction by Michel Kail and Raoul Kirchmayr
Afterword by Fredric Jameson

VERSO
London • New York

The translation of this book was supported by
the Centre National du Livre (CNL)

First published in English by Verso 2016
First published as *Qu'est-ce que la subjectivité?*

1 3 5 7 9 10 8 6 4 2

Verso
UK: 6 Meard Street, London W1F 0EG
US: 388 Atlantic Ave, Brooklyn, NY 11217
versobooks.com

Verso is the imprint of New Left Books

ISBN-13: 978-1-78478-137-8 (PB)
ISBN-13: 978-1-78478-140-8 (HB)
ISBN-13: 978-1-78478-138-5 (US EBK)
ISBN-13: 978-1-78478-139-2 (UK EBK)

British Library Cataloguing in Publication Data
A catalogue record for this book is available from the British Library

Library of Congress Cataloging-in-Publication Data
A catalog record for this book is available from the Library of Congress

Typeset in Sabon MT by Hewer Text UK Ltd, Edinburgh, Scotland
Printed in the United States

Contents

INTRODUCTION:

Consciousness and Subjectivity

By Michel Kail and Raoul Kirchmayr

Sartre gave the talk that you are about to read at Rome's Gramsci Institute in December 1961, not long after he had published his *Critique of Dialectical Reason* in April 1960. This great theoretical work organised a confrontation with Marxism, founded on the paradoxical appreciation that Marxism has come to a standstill[1] *and also* constitutes the unsurpassable horizon of our time.[2]

Why did this lecture take place in Rome and not in Paris? There was next to no chance of Sartre being invited to speak by the French Communist Party (PCF) after his 1956 condemnation of the Soviet invasion of Hungary, whereby he renounced the 'fellow traveller' status that he had taken on in 1952.

---

1 'Marxism has come to a standstill: precisely because this philosophy wants to change the world, because its aim is "philosophy-becoming-the-world", because it is and is intended to be *practical*, a real schism has occurred within it, with the result that theory is rejected on the one hand, and *praxis* on the other', Jean-Paul Sartre, 'Search for a Method', introduction to *Critique of Dialectical Reason*, vol. 1, London: Verso, 2010 [1960], translation altered.

2 '[Marxism] remains, therefore, the philosophy of our time. We cannot go beyond it because we have not gone beyond the circumstances which engendered it . . . But Marx's statement seems to me to point to a factual evidence which we cannot go beyond so long as the transformations of social relations and technical progress have not freed man from the yoke of scarcity', ibid.

Conversely, with its concern for cultural and intellectual openness the Italian Communist Party (PCI) did not fail to pay attention to Sartre's work. The political scientist Marc Lazar has highlighted the fact that while the PCF at best afforded its intellectuals an 'expert' role, the PCI encouraged them to intervene in defining policy itself: 'Despite the conflicts that broke out between the leadership and the intellectuals in certain periods, for instance during the Cold War, these scholars' reflections did contribute to the development of Party policy, especially their elaborations in the context of the Gramsci Institutes. This intellectual presence in the Party leadership – principally meaning the involvement of philosophers and historians – encouraged the flowering of theoretical and cultural discussions therein.[3] The Rome Gramsci Institute in particular served as 'a genuine laboratory of ideas for the Party leadership',[4] so we can understand why such an institute would have been keen to hear the author of the *Critique of Dialectical Reason.*

Right from the start of his intervention, Sartre declared his ambition of putting subjectivity at the heart of Marxist analysis, giving it back its lost energy. At the same time, he mounted a virulent critique of Lukács, whose most important work, *History and Class Consciousness* (1923), many people, then as now, interpreted as having responded to this same ambition.

Lukács's presence in Sartre's reflections is undeniable. Hence in his 'Search for a Method'[5] Sartre made reference to Lukács's *Existentialism or Marxism* (1948),[6] mistakenly citing

---

3 Marc Lazar, *Maisons rouges: Les Partis communistes français et italien de la Libération à nos jours*, Paris: Aubier, 1992, pp. 257–8.

4 Ibid., p. 114.

5 Sartre, 'Search for a Method'.

6 Georg Lukács, 'Existentialism', in *Marxism and Human Liberation: Essays on History, Culture and Revolution by Georg Lukács*, New York: Dell Publishing Co., 1973.

this work as 'Existentialism and Marxism' (a lapsus that is not without a certain charm, and is doubtless also of some significance for our remarks here). In this mediocre text, the Hungarian philosopher denounced existentialism – essentially, Sartre's existentialism – as a new avatar of idealism, which he presented as nothing other than the ideological weapon that the bourgeoisie wields in order to defend its legitimacy. Lukács unconvincingly tried to distance himself from scientism and boasted of having developed a materialism that was free of mechanicism, in that it grasped the essence of realities as they evolved and not statically. Yet this in fact offered no escape from scientism, since for Lukács each stage of this evolution is reflected in consciousness passively.

We ought to note, however, that across the 1960s and 1970s French readers did increasingly turn to Lukács's *History and Class Consciousness*,[7] a work of a wholly different philosophical quality, whose French preface presented it as a 'book that Marxism scorned', in the same category as Karl Korsch's *Marxism and Philosophy*.[8] Both orthodox Marxism – which accused Lukács and Korsch of revisionism, idealism and reformism – and social democracy condemned these works with similar vigour. As Kostas Axelos reminds us, the inspiration for these critiques of Lukács and Korsch was the cult of scientism – the objectivity of the natural sciences – underpinned by a crude realist definition of truth as the adequation of representations to the objects outside of them.

---

7 Georg Lukács, *History and Class Consciousness*, Cambridge, MA: MIT Press, 1971. This work, published in German in 1923, consisted of studies written between 1919 and 1922.

8 Korsch's book also first came out in German in 1923. The first English edition was published by Monthly Review Press in 1970, translated and introduced by Fred Halliday. Reissued by Verso in 2012.

Lukács's project was to capture the *totality* of the social and historical experience that plays out by means of social *praxis* and the class struggle. The category that could be used to understand this process was *mediation*, which establishes the connection between the immediacy caught up in facticity and the totality-in-becoming, allowing for a permanent process of transcendence. The Party, equipped with a 'total conscious will', is able to unite theory and praxis, determining the *form* [*Gestalt*] of proletarian class consciousness. For Lukács, this is connected to an analysis of the *reification* that transforms everything that is into commodities and assigns everything to a 'rationalist pseudo-objectivity' or to an 'idealist pseudo-subjectivity'. The world – the totality engendered by human production – is now foreign to consciousness. The capitalist mode of production drives reification to its paroxysm; the proletariat's task is to put an end to it, through its party.

In the section entitled 'Class Consciousness'[9] Lukács introduces the notion of *objective possibility*: 'By relating consciousness to the whole of society it becomes possible to infer the thoughts and feelings which men would have in a particular situation if they were able to assess both it and the interests arising from it in their impact on immediate action and on the whole structure of society. That is to say, it would be possible to infer the thoughts and feelings appropriate to their objective situation'.[10] The author specifies that such situations present themselves only in limited number, but the appropriate and rational reaction that has to be *imputed* [*zugerechnet*] to this type of situation, fashioned by the process of production, is none other than class consciousness, which determines the

9 Lukács, *History and Class Consciousness*, pp. 46–82.
10 Ibid., p. 51.

historically significant actions of the class as a whole. It is also important not to confuse class consciousness with the psychological consciousness of individual proletarians or proletarians as a mass, since it is 'the sense, become conscious, of the historical role of the class'.[11] Class consciousness belongs to the logic of *imputation*: it is 'imputed' by class interests.[12] Lukács heads his text with a quotation from Marx and Engels that Sartre also cites: 'It is not a question of what this or that proletarian, or even the whole proletariat, at the moment regards as its aim. It is a question of what the proletariat is, and what, in accordance with this being, it will historically be compelled to do'.[13]

These considerations led Lukács to reproach the 'vulgar Marxists' for not having understood that *only* for the proletariat is an understanding of the essence of society a decisively important weapon, and that this exclusivity owes to the 'unique function' that class consciousness fulfils for this class: it gives the proletariat the possibility of apprehending society, from the centre outward, as a coherent whole, and, in tandem with this, the possibility of acting centrally on it; proletarian class consciousness reconciles theory with practice.

In a work in which he mounts a very sharp critique of Sartre,[14] Maurice Merleau-Ponty reserves his favourable

11 Ibid., p. 73

12 *Translator's note*: The English translation of *History and Class Consciousness* refers to 'imputed' consciousness, whereas the French translation cited by the authors of this preface refers to both '*conscience imputée*' and '*conscience adjugée*'. The latter term implies an element of compulsion: for example, in French an *adjudication* can mean, among other things, a forced sale of assets, or an award ordered by a court, and not, as in English, just the fact of the court making the decision.

13 Karl Marx and Friedrich Engels, 'The Holy Family, or Critique of Critical Criticism: Against Bruno Bauer and Company', in *Marx and Engels Collected Works*, vol. 4, London: Lawrence and Wishart, 1975 [1844], p. 37.

14 Maurice Merleau-Ponty, 'Sartre et l'ultra-bolchevisme', in *Les*

comments for Lukács's arguments,[15] congratulating him for his attempt to defend, as against his adversaries, '[a] Marxism that incorporates subjectivity into history without making it its epiphenomenon'.[16]

Sartre could have contented himself with the elements of Lukács's argumentation that we have described and Merleau-Ponty's evaluation of them, thus recognising Lukács as a thinker of subjectivity and an adversary of the Marxism that settles for placing the so-called objective conditions in a supposedly 'dialectical' movement. All the more so because Sartre emphasised the pertinence of Lukács's diagnosis of the Marxism that had come to a standstill – a voluntaristic idealism – and also shared the Hungarian philosopher's themes of consciousness and totality.

So where did Sartre's reticence come from? In his lecture Sartre presents subjectivity in terms of its two traits of both 'not-knowing' and 'having-to-be'. These were two characteristics familiar to readers of *The Transcendence of the Ego* (1936) and *Being and Nothingness* (1943), leaving no doubt as to the remarkable continuity in the intuitions that inspired Sartre's work.

Sartre placed emphasis on not-knowing in order to deconstruct the privileged status that the philosophy of the subject had accorded to reflection, which it posed as characteristic of consciousness. The French philosopher stressed that consciousness is by definition self-consciousness, *and therefore* a nonreflective self-consciousness; otherwise, given that reflected self-consciousness is intermittent, we would have to accept the absurdity that in between moments of reflection there is an

---

Aventures de la dialectique, Paris: Gallimard, 1955, pp. 131–271.

15 'Le marxisme "occidental"', in ibid., pp. 43–80.

16 Ibid., p. 57.

unconscious consciousness. In other words, self-consciousness is not self-knowledge. Having-to-be is the mode of being of consciousness, which is thus existent. While the subject *is*, consciousness is not borne by any being, for as Sartre makes clear, it is an absolute: an absolute of existence. Most important, consciousness is not the consciousness of a subject. If that were the case, it would surely have no function other than to reflect the subject's being (in the philosophy of the subject, consciousness of the self is necessarily a *reflected* consciousness of the self, that is, a consciousness that refers back to the subject's own being). Consciousness is not the consciousness of a subject, since in the conceptual order that Sartre elaborates, consciousness is substituted for the concept of the subject. This formulation, too, is an approximate one, since consciousness does not occupy the subject's place, but rather redefines the geography established by the philosophy of the subject. This is what goes unconsidered by those authors who incautiously remark that Sartre injected a dose of subjectivity into a dolefully objectivist environment.

Having-to-be is a theme that places Sartre's reflection in a resolutely antinaturalist perspective – a perspective that Simone de Beauvoir had already explored in all its depth in her masterpiece *The Second Sex*. Needless to say, Sartre's having-to-be does not enter into Aristotle's schema of potential and act, which requires the prior posing of a possible that bears all the determinations of being except for realisation. Enclosed within this possible being – which, in the famous theory of four causes, is assumed by the formal cause – is an essence: 'Essence is the first inner principle of all that belongs to the possibility of a thing'.[17]

17 Immanuel Kant, *Metaphysical Foundations of Natural Science*, ed. Michael Friedman, Cambridge: Cambridge University Press, 2004, p. 3.

Essentialism commands a specific articulation of the necessary, the real and the possible. Since essence circumscribes the possible being, it is none other than the principle of being; it is prior to it in law and in deed. The real is, then, confined to an intermediary role: it is the field in which necessity deploys its effects, thus revealing its coincidence with the possible. It is restricted to the role of a testing ground, or an opportunity: the opportunity for the actualisation of a potentiality. Sartre was clear about his disagreement on this point: 'Being-in-itself can not "be potentiality" or "have potentialities". In itself it is what it is, in the absolute plenitude of its identity. The cloud is not "potential rain"; it is, in itself, a certain quantity of water vapour, which at a given temperature and under a given pressure is strictly what it is. The in-itself is actuality'.[18] So if there is a world of the possible, it must be introduced by a being that is itself its own possibility: being-for-itself, consciousness.

It is particularly telling that, in this lecture, Sartre was so concerned to shine a light on the link between not-knowing, or prereflective self-consciousness, and having-to-be, at the precise moment when his intention was to define the *materialist* status of subjectivity. As he explains, 'This is the first essential characteristic of subjectivity: if subjectivity is, by definition, non-knowledge, even at the level of consciousness, it is because the individual – the organism – has to be his being'. This allows for just two possibilities, Sartre adds. One consists of being one's material being, as in the (extreme) case of a pure material system – here there is the deficit, and that is all; the other concerns modifying the whole in order to ensure one's own maintenance, as in the case of *praxis*. Between the two there is

18 Jean-Paul Sartre, *Being and Nothingness*, trans. Hazel E. Barnes, New York: Philosophical Library, 1956, p. 98. Translation modified.

the *condition of interiority*, in the sense that the whole is not something already given that has to be preserved when it is threatened, but something that *always* has to be preserved, because it is never definitively given.

So Sartre proposes, on the one hand, that interiority is a condition, and on the other hand that the whole has to be; in other words, that it is always on course to totalisation, including when we are talking about an organic whole. These two propositions lead us to the recognition that interiority is what we could call a 'conditioned-condition'. It is *conditioned* because the whole, which is not given, can only persist if it is driven by a tendency that is at one with the construction of the whole:

> In reality, the whole is a law of interiorisation and perpetual reorganisation. In other words, the organism is first and foremost a totalisation, more than a whole; the whole can only be a kind of self-regulation that perpetually brings with it this interiorisation as totalisation. Totalisation occurs through the integration of an outside that disturbs and changes; and the hemianopic is an example of this. All in all, the whole is no different from the overall drive. The drive and the need are at one. We cannot say that there are needs first; there is one need, which is the organism itself as a requirement to survive.

This conditioning of interiority ought not be translated into determinist terms, which would suppose that the whole is definite, and confers such and such content on interiority; rather, it ought to be understood as drawing on interiority – or better, the interiorisation process – with a view to its own continuation as a totalisation in progress. Having-to-be, interiorisation and totalisation are so many synonyms and belong to the order of existence.[19] 'Now this practical, dialectical unity that haunts the group and causes it to negate it in its very effort at integration, is simply what we have elsewhere called existence'.[20]

These considerations should doubtless suffice for a better appreciation of the interest and present-day relevance of Sartre's lecture. To this end it is interesting also to consider the discussion that Sartre's argumentation roused among the Italian intellectuals who attended his talk. The more phenomenologically minded ones followed Sartre the whole way and perfectly understood the true significance of his presentation – as Valentini's intervention, for example, demonstrates. But most of them, despite certainly being attentive to Sartre's philosophical discourse (which, we repeat, distinguished them from the French Communists), were unable to free themselves from the idea – or rather, feeling – that abandoning an objectivist posture meant reneging on a materialist stance and submitting to bourgeois ideology.[21] So they accepted a dose of subjectivism but without being able to renounce the objectivist foundation of materialism and (in tandem with this) being able to understand that they remained prisoners of the dualism of subject and

---

19 In order to cast aside any confusion, it is worth emphasising that Sartre's argument defining the status of subjectivity is formulated on the basis of a critique that he repeats throughout the *Critique of Dialectical Reason*, targeting the 'organicist illusion', which is a constant temptation for the group. 'The group is haunted by organicist meanings because it is subject to this rigorous law [of a perpetually reworked and perpetually incomplete totalisation]: if it did succeed in reaching organic unity – but this is impossible – then it would thus be a hyperorganism (because it would be an organism producing itself according to a practical law that excluded contingency); but because it is rigorously forbidden from achieving this status, it remains *a totalisation and a being* on this side [*en deçà*] of the practical organism, and one of its products' (Jean-Paul Sartre, *Critique of Dialectical Reason*, London: NLB, 1976, p. 538, translation edited.)

20 Sartre, *Critique of Dialectical Reason*, p. 563, translation edited.

21 The discussion of poetry is particularly interesting in this regard.

object. They could be responsive to the Hegelian solution that Lukács proposed, in that it allowed them to continue to believe in this dualism while also serenely envisaging its transcendence – since, as we know, a dialectical transcendence preserves the thing that has been transcended. An important reason for such an attachment to objectivism was the attempt to disarm the threat of antinaturalism, which seemed to tend towards derealisation in its insistence on denaturalisation. This despite the fact that antinaturalism does not at all hold that nothing is given; rather, it insists that this given must not be interpreted in terms of nature, and emphasises that the given is infinitely richer when these terms are not used since, as we have indicated, it is relational.

Sartre, for his part, was clear that Lukács had fallen into an excessive Hegelianism. Notwithstanding his stated rejection of objectivism, he continued to think history with the assistance of the regulating idea of a philosophy of history, which orders real history according to the principle of transcendentalism, much as Kant's argumentation arranged phenomena in terms of categories of understanding. The philosophy of history anticipates real history once and for all: it delimits the possibility of this history, and is this history in its essentiality. Only with reference to the philosophy of history is it possible to construct and legitimise the notion of 'objective possibility'. Subjectivity is thus convoked (this term's use here also bearing a tone of 'assignation') in the name of imputed [*imputée ou adjugée*] 'class consciousness', under the pretext of actualising the possibility traced in the sky by the philosophy of history. Consciousness – in this case, proletarian consciousness – has to be this possible consciousness that the philosophy of history reserves for it. '[W]e must never overlook the distance that separates the consciousness of even the most revolutionary worker from the authentic class consciousness of the proletariat.[22]

Consciousness's having-to-be, as described by Lukács, is very different from the having-to-be that is constitutive of consciousness's being according to Sartre: for Lukács, what proletarian consciousness has to be is outside of it, a norm that it has to attain. The place that the production process assigns (second assignation) to the proletariat thus gives notice for proletarian consciousness. That is to say, such consciousness is narrowly framed by the base, through economic determinism, and from above, by the ideal of possible consciousness. How can we imagine such a consciousness having the power to extirpate itself of its real in order to coincide with its possibility? Lukács's answer in this regard evokes 'the question of the proletariat's internal transformation'.[23] However, the conceptual frame within which he traps consciousness leaves it next to no room to show any kind of autonomy. Moreover, in 'Reification and the Class Consciousness of the Proletariat', his book's central chapter, Lukács cloisters consciousness's activity within very narrow limits (wholly in concordance with the presuppositions of his analysis, we might add), writing that it

> is by no means the invention of the proletariat, nor was it 'created' out of the void. It is rather the *inevitable consequence of the process in its totality*; one which changed from being an abstract possibility to a concrete reality only after it had become part of the consciousness of the proletariat and had been made practical by it. And this is no mere formal transformation. *For a possibility to be realised, for a tendency*

22 Lukács, *History and Class Consciousness*, p. 80.
23 Ibid.

> *to become actual*, what is required is that the objective components of a society should be transformed; their functions must be changed and with them the structure and content of every individual object.[24]

The formulas that we have italicised here have no meaning or function other than to resolve the problem before it has even been posed – in sum, to get around it.

Lukács could not conceive of history without the presupposition of a philosophy of history, of an already closed totality, of a totality of possibles awaiting actualisation. Confronted with such a totality, subjectivity is, then, conceived in the terms of the classic philosophy of the subject: that is, the terms of reflexivity, which must assume – even if dialectically – that this totality *is*. When Sartre characterises Lukács's argumentation as an 'idealist dialectics', he means that in the sense that this dialectic is deprived of any real effectiveness, because it guarantees only the actualisation of a totality that is already there, confining subjectivity to the role of spectator of a predetermined process. Moreover, he criticises Lukács's 'voluntaristic idealism' because it can allow subjectivity to intervene only insofar as it stoically acquiesces to the dual necessity that a philosophy of history has already set in place, prior to subjectivity entering the stage. With Sartre having already demonstrated that will comes second to freedom, the valorisation of the former can only be to the detriment of the latter. And this defines the voluntarism whose vacuity Sartre makes so apparent.[25]

---

24 Ibid., pp. 204–5; our italics.

25 'The will, far from being the unique or at least the privileged manifestation of freedom, actually – like every event of the for-itself – must presuppose the foundation of an original freedom in order to be able

Let us now try to pair this theoretical insight with a political one.

The bourgeoisie established itself as an emancipatory class, denigrating the privileges that the nobility had granted itself on a hereditary basis. Yet that did not mean that the bourgeoisie put an end to privileges.

De Beauvoir thus explained in the foreword to *Privilèges* that

> although these essays were written in different times and perspectives, they respond to one same question: how can the privileged think their situation? The old nobility [*ancien noblesse*] was ignorant of such a problem: it defended its rights, exercising them without worrying about legitimising them. The rising bourgeoisie, on the contrary, forged itself an ideology appropriate for its liberation; having become a ruling class, it could hardly repudiate this heritage. But all thought is directed towards universality, and it is no simple enterprise to make a universal justification for the possession of particular advantages.[26]

---

to constitute itself as will. The will in fact is posited as a reflective decision in relation to certain ends. But it does not create these ends': Sartre, *Being and Nothingness*, p. 443. Isolated from this original freedom, will is incapable of bringing about these ends by itself, because its only competence is that of managing the means, such that it recognises the order of truths and values supported by the divine will or responds to the demands of a supposedly necessary economic order. The political voluntarism that some count on to restore the prestige of politics is in truth a synonym for impotence and submission to a transcendent order, be it from above (the divine) or from below (the natural).

26 Simone de Beauvoir, *Privilèges*, Paris: Gallimard, 1955, p. 7. On this notion of privilege, and the differentiated use that De Beauvoir makes of it, see Geneviève Fraisse, *Le Privilège de Simone de Beauvoir (suivi de Une mort douce)*, Arles: Actes Sud, 2008. See also our review of this work: Michel Kail, *Travail, Genre et Sociétés*, Paris: La Découverte, 2012/2, no. 28, pp. 212–14.

The perspective of the universal introduced uncertainty as to the legitimacy of the bourgeoisie's dominant position. The temptation, then, is to point an accusing finger at the contradiction between the bourgeoisie's emancipatory vocation – which articulated its self-consciousness around the universalism of Enlightenment philosophy – and its dominant position, guaranteeing the satisfaction of its particular, selfish interests. But that is to expect more from the logic of emancipation than it can consequentially produce. This is a dual logic, and it can be set to work only by an emancipator that accords freedom to the persons it judges worthy of being emancipated, according to criteria of its own. The candidate for freedom thus receives a freedom that has the status of an accorded quality, and not that of the being of a consciousness that has to be. Here the emancipated is a subject in both senses of the term: first, that of a being capable of using freedom (the instrument that emancipation has provided it); and second, that of a vassal subject, like a king's subject, and now the subject of the emancipator. It is in this sense that the emancipator's conservation of his privileges conforms to the logic of emancipation. The norm of emancipation gravitates around the same conceptual framework as does the 'subject' in the philosophy of the subject, effectively reduced to being a support for a series of qualities or attributes, including freedom. The emancipator can give freedom to this or that subject just as the politician pins the Order of Merit on the lapel of the devoted collaborator's jacket. Freedom is thus reduced to the level of will and condemned to the impotence of voluntarism.

If this logic is to be disturbed, it is necessary to appeal to a new and different logic: the logic of self-emancipation. Antinaturalism is the philosophical prerequisite for this logic: here the (self-) emancipated being constructs itself in and through the emancipation process, and is not – as in the logic of emancipation – earlier anticipated by the emancipatory will of the emancipator, or by a possibility prescribed by some sort of philosophy of history. More precisely, the logic of self-emancipation requires the antinaturalist materialism that Sartre is here elaborating, in which the materialist dimension serves to identify a situation of exploitation, and the a-naturalist dimension to leave it to an act of freedom to designate what is possible. These two moments cannot be spread out in time, but rather must be convoked simultaneously. Marxism can mark out an unsurpassable horizon to the extent that it is understood as the opportunity to pose the question of materialism itself – which, as Sartre warns us, can only bear its full fruits if it is inspired by an intransigent antinaturalist stance. It is not enough to graft subjectivity onto the body of Marxism, which can always lead to incompatibility. Rather, it is necessary to re-found Marxism on the basis of an antinaturalist understanding of subjectivity, so that materialist philosophy remains faithful to its vocation: that of a philosophy of freedom.

A Note to the New edition

There have already been two publications[1] based on the lecture that Sartre gave in Rome on 12 December 1961, as part of his 12–14 December meeting at the Gramsci Institute with PCI intellectuals and others close to the PCI. The first of these was in Italian, appearing in *Aut Aut* journal (no. 136–7, July–October 1973) under the title 'Soggettività e marxismo';[2] the second was in French, appearing in Sartre's journal *Les Temps modernes* (no. 560, March 1993) under the title 'La Conference de Rome, 1961: Marxisme et subjectivité'.[3] These two versions were established independently of one another, on the basis of the transcription of the recording of Sartre's lecture, with the editors of *Aut Aut* offering an Italian translation. For the *Les Temps modernes* version we (MK) also used this transcription,

1 An English translation of Sartre's lecture as well as the postface by Fredric Jameson both appeared in *New Left Review* 2:88, 2015. This English translation was based on the 2013 French edition (Paris: Les Prairies Ordinaires), edited by Michel Kail and Raoul Kirchmayr.

2 Founded in 1951, *Aut Aut* is a prestigious Italian philosophy journal whose current editor-in-chief is Pier Aldo Rovatti. The issue containing the text of Sartre's lecture is presented as a '*fascicolo speciale*', with the title 'Sartre dopo la Critique'. Sartre's text appears on pp. 133–51 and a few elements of the discussion that followed on pp. 152–8.

3 With an introduction by Michel Kail, 'Introduction à la conférence de Sartre: La conscience n'est pas sujet' (pp. 1–10) and followed by some remarks by Tibor Szabó ('Note annexe: Sartre, l'Italie et la subjectivité' pp. 40–41). We would like to take the opportunity to warmly thank Claude Lanzmann, the director of the journal, for generously allowing us to republish this text in the present edition.

which was entrusted to us by the Hungarian philosopher Tibor Szabó, though we also added in a few syntactical changes to make it easier to read. The differences between the two versions are minimal and are not cause for divergent interpretations.

Even if in the strict sense this is not a Sartre text – since the manuscript either no longer exists, or remains impossible to find, and the tape of Sartre's lecture is lost – its reasoning and its thematic are, nonetheless, very much those of a text of his.

So why this new edition, after the text has already been published in both French and Italian? Subsequent to the appearance of both versions, we got access to a new element, namely the transcription of the discussions sparked by Sartre's lecture. These discussions continued throughout the whole of 12 December and the mornings of each of the following two days, with interventions by Paci, Luporini, Lombardo-Radice, Colletti, Della Volpe, Valentini, Semerari, Piovene, Alicata, and Cardona, as well as Sartre's own responses.[4] It seems that most of Sartre's interlocutors made their interventions in French – in a few cases, they apologised to Sartre for instead making their points in Italian – meaning that the Italian-language transcription of the debates is for the most part a translation. Our retranslation back from the Italian has sought to respect the spirit of these interventions, perhaps sometimes to the detriment of sticking to the letter of the text.

We are not publishing the whole discussion, which would have made for rather too thick a volume. Our criterion in choosing the texts has been to retain the elements and moments of

4 The tape of these exchanges is also lost. Many thanks to Paolo Tamassia for recovering the typescript of these discussions at the Gramsci Institute, and for entrusting the text to us; and to Gabriella Farina for helping us in our exchanges with the Institute. Both are eminent representatives of Sartre studies in Italy.

the discussion that help further clarify Sartre's reasoning, and even to enrich it. Given this criterion, we have left aside the interventions that seemed digressive, or which looked too much like debates internal to Italian intellectuals.[5]

5 Here we would like to thank our publisher Nicolas Vieillescazes, a driving force behind this publication, who contributed to this project with very useful assistance and great enthusiasm.

MARXISM AND SUBJECTIVITY: JEAN-PAUL SARTRE'S ROME LECTURE

MARXISM AND SUBJECTIVITY:

Jean-Paul Sartre's Rome Lecture

Our problem here is that of subjectivity in the context of Marxist philosophy. My aim is to establish with precision whether the principles and truths that constitute Marxism allow subjectivity to exist and have a function, or whether they reduce it to a set of facts that can be ignored in the dialectical study of human development. Taking Lukács as an example, I hope to convince you that an erroneous interpretation of certain undoubtedly ambiguous Marxist texts can give rise to what I would call an 'idealist dialectics', which in practice ignores the subject, and to show how such a position may be damaging for the development of Marxist studies. My topic is not subject and object, but rather subjectivity, or subjectivation, and objectivity or objectivation. The subject is a different, far more complex problem. When I speak of subjectivity, it is as a certain type of internal action, an interior system – *système en intériorité* – rather than the simple, immediate relationship of the subject to itself.

A superficial consideration of Marxist philosophy might tempt us to call it 'pan-objectivism', insofar as the Marxist dialectician is, it seems, interested only in objective reality. Some of Marx's writings can be interpreted in this way, such as the well-known passage from *The Holy Family*: 'The question is not what this or that proletarian, or even the whole of the proletariat at the moment considers as its aim. The question is what the proletariat is, and what, consequent on that *being*, it will be compelled to do."[1] The subjective is thus pushed into the category of representation, which, taken in itself, is of no importance, underlying reality being merged with the process that makes the proletariat the agent of the destruction of the bourgeoisie and constrains it to be this agent in reality – that is, objectively, in actual fact. Other writings go further still, suggesting that the subjective lacks even the importance of a representation belonging to the subject or to a group of individuals, since it disappears completely as such. We need only recall this passage from *Capital*:

> The belated scientific discovery that the products of labour, in so far as they are values, are merely the material expressions of the human labour expended to produce them, marks an epoch in the history of mankind's development, but by no means banishes the semblance of objectivity possessed by the social characteristics of labour. Something which is only valid for this particular form of production, the production of commodities, namely the fact that the specific social character of private labours carried on independently of each other consists in their equality as human labour, and, in the product, assumes the form of the existence of value, appears to those caught up in the relations of commodity production (and this is true both before and after the above-mentioned scientific discovery) to be just as ultimately valid as the fact that the scientific dissection of the air into its component parts left the atmosphere itself unaltered in its physical configuration.[2]

1 *The Holy Family*, trans. R. Dixon, Moscow: Foreign Languages Publishing House, 1956, p. 53.

2 Karl Marx, *Capital*, vol. 1, Harmondsworth: Penguin, 1976, p. 167.

Against Lukács

It seems there is no difficulty here, since everyone agrees on this point. However, the ambiguity of the phrasing deceived some, notably Lukács. This is because in this text subjectivity seems to disappear completely. Appearances are as objective and real as their underlying ground, produced as they are by the economic process itself. The same is true of reification, which is an element produced by the process of capital, and of the fetishisation of commodities, which is its direct result. So when we apprehend a particular commodity as a fetish, although we have been forewarned by Marxist theory, we settle for doing what reality demands of us, since, at a certain level this commodity is objectively and really fetishised. It is then that subjective reality seems to fade away, since the 'carrier' of economic relations realises them where he is, as he must realise them, his idea of them being confined to reflecting them at the level of his *praxis*. This is why a thinker like Lukács can advance a theory of entirely objective class consciousness. Although he takes subjectivity as his starting point, it is solely to relate it to the individual subject, understood as a source of errors, or simply inadequate realisation. He then regards class consciousness as more or less well developed, more or less clear or obscure, more or less contradictory, more or less effective, according to whether or not the class being analysed belongs directly to the fundamental process of production. For example, in a petty bourgeois, class consciousness remains objectively vague and, for reasons Lukács sets out, never forms into real class consciousness, whereas the proletariat, being deeply involved in the production process, can be brought to a complete form of class consciousness through the objective reality of work.

So, this conception pushes objectivism to the point where it obliterates all subjectivity and hence leads us into idealism.

This is no doubt a dialectical idealism, with material conditions as its starting point, but it is still idealism. Neither Marx himself nor Marxism lend themselves to this. There are texts that are indeed ambiguous – by virtue of their depth – but none of them can be interpreted as though pan-objectivism were the goal of Marxism. When Marx speaks of 'existence' – as he does, say, in the 1857 draft 'Introduction' to his critique of political economy[3] – he has in mind the total man, a being defined by a dialectic with three terms: need, work and enjoyment. So if we want to use Marx to understand the dialectics of production as a whole, we must first return to its ground, and to the being who has needs and seeks to meet them, in other words to produce and reproduce his life through work, and who, through the resulting economic process, attains more or less complete enjoyment.

If we take these three elements into account, we note first that the three together establish a rigorous connection between a real man and a real society and the surrounding material reality that is not himself. This is a synthetic connection between the man and the material world and, in and through this connection, it is also a mediated relationship between human beings. In other words, in this very text, the reality of human beings is theorised and linked to transcendence, to a beyond, to what is outside and before them. Human beings need something that is not them. The organism needs oxygen and this already constitutes a relationship with the surroundings, with transcendence. A man works to obtain tools that will enable him to appease his hunger and reproduces his existence in some form that depends on economic development.

3 Karl Marx, *Grundrisse: Foundations of the Critique of Political Economy (Rough Draft)*, Harmondsworth: Penguin, 1973, p. 106.

Here again, need is an element located elsewhere, and enjoyment is an incorporation through certain internal processes of what this man needs, which is precisely external being. The first connection Marx reveals through these three terms is a connection with *outside being*, which we call transcendence. The three elements form a kind of explosion of the self into 'outside being' and, at the same time, a return to and re-appropriation of the self. As such these three terms can be objectively described and, at a particular level, can be an object of knowledge. But, through a regressive analysis, they are equally related to something like a self, which denies and goes beyond itself while conserving itself. To use Marx's terms, since work is objectivation through the reproduction of life, we are entitled to ask who and what is objectified through work? Who or what is threatened by need? Who or what puts an end to need through enjoyment? The answer, obviously, is the practical, biological organism or – if we prefer, considering subjectivity – the psychosomatic unit. So now we are dealing with a reality that exceeds direct knowledge of the self through interiority.

Importance of not knowing

Let us suppose that work is carried out using a tool; there is a practical surpassing of the situation towards a goal, which implies knowledge of the goal and of the means, of the nature of the materials, of the inert requirements of the tool and, in a capitalist society, of the factory where the individual works, its standards and so on. So many different aspects of knowledge are involved here, and this knowledge is at once organic and practical, since in some cases it can be acquired by training. However, the positions we must adopt to hold the tool and use the materials are not a matter of knowledge, still less the muscles, bones and nerve links that make it possible to hold this or that position. In other words, there is an objectivity maintained by something that is beyond knowledge, and which, moreover, it might be practically detrimental to know. Let us take a well-known example: if, as you go downstairs, you become conscious of what you are doing and if consciousness emerges to determine what you do, to intervene in this action, you immediately stumble because the action no longer has the character it should.

We can thus observe that, even in cases where the division of labour in society extends to machines and where, consequently, semi-automatic machines impose piecemeal tasks on the worker, the simplest movement that a worker is asked to do is one that does not engender knowledge of the body. The required movement can be demonstrated, but the organic reality of moving, altering position and changing the whole according to the part is not directly a matter of knowledge. Why? Because we are in the presence of a system which, for reasons we shall examine, has non-knowledge as a component part and whose parts no longer appear in transcendence, but in interiority.

Let us establish a clear definition of what we understand by a *system in interiority*, for the sake of a better understanding of what we are talking about. A material system is defined as having an *interior* or, if you prefer, as marking off a domain within the real world, when the relationship between its parts involves the relation of each to the whole. Reciprocally, the whole is no more than the sum of its parts insofar as it is involved as a whole in the relations that the parts have with each other. Of course, the recognition of our organic status as a system of interiority should not lead us to forget that we are also defined by inorganic status. In this regard it is possible to understand us as a set of cells. This is what we are doing when we say that a human organism contains 80–90 per cent water. The same is true when we are subject to mechanical forces. It must also be said that the organic is not a set of specific objects in nature that supplement the inorganic, but corresponds to the particular status of certain inorganic wholes; it is a status defined by the interiorisation of the outside. This means that what the organism experiences in the form of a relation of interiority can also be understood as a physico-chemical whole. It is as though the entire physico-chemical whole were not sufficiently determined and, in some areas or sectors, this whole in exteriority can also be defined by a law in interiority.

So, at the outset at least, we can then identify two types of exteriority: first, the exteriority of within or, if you prefer, 'on this side' – *en deçà* – or 'before'; in other words, a type of exteriority whose crowning feature is organic status, from which death can return us to the inorganic. Second, the exteriority of 'beyond' – *au-delà* – which reflects what this organism finds in front of it as a work object, a need and the means to satisfy it, in order to maintain its status as an organism. Thus, we have a dialectic with three terms. This requires us to describe interiorisation of the exterior by the organism, in order to understand its capacity to re-exteriorise in transcendent being, in carrying out an act of work or determining a need. So there is only one moment called *interiority*, which is a kind of mediation between two moments of transcendent being.

However, we should not think that these two moments are in themselves necessarily distinct, other than for temporal reasons. Ultimately it is the same being, the same being in exteriority, which mediates with itself, and it is this that is *interiority*. As this mediation defines the space in which the unity of two types of exteriority will occur, it is necessarily immediate to itself in the sense that it does not contain its own knowledge. Consequently, it is at the level of this mediation, which is not itself mediated, that we encounter pure subjectivity. And it is from this starting point, taking account of a number of Marxist themes, that we need to reach a better understanding of the status of this mediation. Does it have a role in human development as a whole? Does it really exist as an indispensable moment in a dialectic crowned by objective knowledge? Or is it merely an epiphenomenon? In putting these questions, we are not bringing in from outside a notion of subjectivity that is not present in Marx; on the contrary we are rendering explicit and taking up a notion that was already given in Marxism itself with the concepts of need, work and enjoyment, even though it went unrecognised by some idealist objectivists such as Lukács.

The anti-Semite

Why, first of all, must this mediation, which is immediate to itself, imply non-knowledge as its particular characteristic? Why must we in our *praxis* – which is knowledge and action together, action that engenders its own understanding – why, at the level of what we call subjectivity, must we also be non-knowing of ourselves? We shall also consider how, in these conditions, we can attain subjectivity, since, if subjectivity is in practice a non-object, if, as such, it escapes knowledge, how can we claim to state any truths about it?

All this can be clarified very simply, but only on the basis of extremely simple situations. Let us take the case of the anti-Semite. An anti-Semite, a man who hates Jews, is an enemy of Jews. But it is also fairly common for anti-Semites not to declare themselves as such. In the context of a mass social movement, such as the one fostered by the Nazis in 1933, he may find the courage to state his position: 'I hate Jews'. But otherwise he does not behave like that. He says, 'Anti-Semitic? Me? No, I'm not anti-Semitic, I just think that Jews have this or that fault and that, consequently, it's better to prevent them getting involved in politics and to restrict their commercial contact with non-Jews, because there's something corrupting about them', and so on. In short, this man presents us with the character of a Jew, which he claims to understand, but he does it insofar as he himself does not understand that he is anti-Semitic. This is the first stage. We have all met people who have said the nastiest, most disagreeable things possible about Jews, while claiming that they are doing so in the name of objectivity, not subjectivity. A little while ago a friend of mine, a Communist friend – Morange in Paris – told me that long before the war he was in a Party cell where one worker systematically opposed everything he said. This was not in any way an ordinary discussion, although one could have taken place. It was not a manifestation of incompatibility between a manual worker and an intellectual, as sometimes happens, since in the same cell there were other intellectuals with whom this worker got on very well. The worker said, 'It was really a physical thing, I just don't like him!' One day, this worker went to see him and said: 'Listen, I've realised why I didn't like you all that time, it's because you're Jewish, and now I realise that it was because I hadn't got rid of some of the prejudices that are part of bourgeois ideology. I didn't see that at first and your example has helped me. I've realised that it's the Jew that I hate in you, because I'm anti-Semitic.'

Note the change. At this moment a kind of contradiction between a general attitude and a particular attitude – a contradiction which, unfortunately does not work in the case of a petty bourgeois on whom there is no brake acting to prevent him expressing his anti-Semitism – a contradiction between general communist humanism and a particular attitude leads to a considered realisation. But you will note that at this moment anti-Semitism as such is being eradicated. True, there is a passage to the object, but it is at the moment when the worker recognises his anti-Semitism that he is very close to shedding it. He may find this difficult, he may think he has shed it but fall back into it in the end. But ultimately he is nevertheless close to shedding it, because anti-Semitism is no longer the subjective construction of an object, a relation of the *inside* and *outside* with an *inside* that does not know itself; it suddenly becomes an object before his eyes, before the conscious thought of the person practising it. Of course, he is then free to make his choice accordingly. This distinction between the anti-Semite as subjectivity apprehending an object that is the Jew and an anti-Semite reflecting on and apprehending himself as an anti-Semitic object has something truly destructive for the subjective itself.

What has really happened? This man did not know that he was anti-Semitic, just as we do not know that there is oil beneath the surface in a particular region or that there is a particular star that we have not yet discovered. And, just as one day we can discover the reservoir of oil or the star, so a man can discover that he is anti-Semitic. But we need to examine this more closely. In the case of anti-Semitism, discovering it means discovering a 'reservoir' that is a residue of bourgeois ideology, in order to eradicate it. But the knowledge connection established between the discovered star and the astronomer does not alter the star in any way. Were we to suppose that this relationship did alter it, we should be falling into idealism in one way or another, insofar as we would be thinking that, in itself, discovery through knowledge acts on the object that is known. In reality, discovery through knowledge establishes a connection of exteriority with the known object, a connection that does not abolish distance. Of course there is an element of interiority in play; but because knowledge seeks to match an idea to its object, the more it develops the more its difference from the known object diminishes. We could even say metaphorically that perfect knowledge would be the object functioning with the subject inside it making it function. Perfect knowledge of an oil well is the oil well. There is no alteration.

If, on the other hand, we consider the action of knowledge on the worker who had previously 'innocently' been anti-Semitic, we can see that it radically transforms the known object insofar as he is obliged either to stop accepting that he is a Communist worker, or to stop accepting that he is an anti-Semite. Something has happened that has completely transformed him. He has built up two systems – in other words, he has summed up his Jewish comrade in exteriority by saying he is Jewish, and he has just summed himself up by saying 'I am anti-Semitic.' The words go far beyond the work he has done on himself; they reclassify him, establish him in objectivity as part of a group and introduce an axiological system of values, which promises him a future and enables him to commit himself. If he is anti-Semitic, that means he hates all Jews and that next week, if he meets one, he will detest him. In value terms this means that he is not the man who shares the values of his comrades, since, on the contrary, in the name of their values he is himself condemned.

This second stage, this second totalisation, leads to commitment, to objective conduct; it involves a value judgement, appears as a relationship to the entire community and puts the future at risk. Gone is the time of subjectivity, when the only object was the individual taken for a Jew. Does this mean that he was not anti-Semitic when he did that? Naturally, insofar as we understand that he retained within him a residue of bourgeois society, of bourgeois ideology that he had not managed to dispel, then yes, he was. But insofar as there was a 'reservoir' within him that made him anti-Semitic, then no, he was not. He was simply making a subjective attempt to orientate himself in a world he did not understand, which eluded his own knowledge, his own distance from himself and his own commitment. So we can see that the appearance of the subjectivity-object to the subject himself leads to its transformation.

'Love' in Stendhal

Stendhal's novels offer two celebrated examples of this. In the first, from *The Charterhouse of Parma*, Count Mosca, who is in love with La Sanseverina, sees her leaving with her handsome young nephew Fabrice to spend two weeks at Lake Como. The pair share affectionate, somewhat ambiguous feelings, and as he watches them leave he thinks: if the word 'love' passes between them I am lost. In other words, if this feeling – which is unknown, not yet to be known, unnamed – acquires a name, I am lost because this naming is bound to lead to specific behaviour and commitments that will mean they will feel obliged to love each other. *The Red and the Black* proposes a contrasting situation. Why does Mme de Rénal give herself to Julien Sorel when she abhors adultery? It is because she does not understand what love is; she cannot put the name 'love' to what is happening inside her, because love has been defined for her by Jesuits who have experienced it only in books, in the context of casuistry. Furthermore, other men – friends of her husband, and neither young nor handsome – have tried to draw her into adultery, to her horror.

Thus, her conception of love so named means that the emotions she feels in relation to this very young man, her children's tutor, cannot be regarded as love. These feelings are something quite different for her; she simply experiences them. The time will come when she does give them this name, because she begins to make love's gestures. If someone had told her, 'It's love', she would have put an end to the relationship. But this did not happen. Thus, the situation illustrates the fact that subjective knowledge constantly transforms its object. Hence also the significance of this moment for subjectivity: how the movement to objectivity alters it – whereas if we name a star we do not alter it – and, consequently, the importance of non-knowledge, or the immediate within mediation.

A second question will help us understand the functional importance of non-knowledge. If it is true that the psychosomatic unit performs a subjective interiorisation of external being, following which there is a practical negation as a result of which it works on the external being that is placed before it; and if, furthermore, there is a constant transformation of this subjectivity as soon as we have knowledge of it, how can we hope to utter any truth in its regard, or even seek to utter any truth? Every time we try, we will distort it. So how is it, consequently, that we can speak about subjectivity without making it into an object? If subjectivity is apprehended where it happens, in the form of an interiorisation of the exterior, a transformation of a system of exteriorisation into a system of interiorisation, it is distorted; it becomes an object external to me, I hold it at a distance. Where I can recognise it better is in the results of work and *praxis*, in response to a situation. If subjectivity can be revealed to me, it is due to a difference between what the situation usually demands and the response I make to it. We should not believe that this differentiation is necessarily a lesser response; it may be something richer, which will carry on developing. In any case, if we regard the situation as a test, of whatever kind, it requires something of the subject. The response will never be totally appropriate to the objective demand; it will either go beyond it or will not be located precisely where necessary; it will fall to one side or fall short. So it is in the response itself that we can apprehend what subjectivity is. Subjectivity is outside, in keeping with the nature of a response and, to the extent that it is constituted as an object, with the nature of the object.

Forms of adaptation

To develop this idea at greater length, let us first consider a medical case: the response of someone suffering from hemianopia, half-blindness. This case is interesting to us because, although it undoubtedly relates to a psychosomatic unit, it is as close as possible to a simple organic connection, involving a lesion that affects the optic nerve where it joins the lobes of the brain. In certain cases, this lesion causes a dysfunction such that half the visual field of each eye is blind and the image forms on only half of the retina. But because the eye is an organisation, the retina's reactions are built up around a central point in the middle of what is called the macula, or yellow spot, a region where retinal images form most clearly. If we were dealing with a strictly inorganic, entirely external system, the consequence of this hemianopic deficit would be a vision of reality reduced by half. Let us imagine for a moment that I could cause the same lesion deliberately, as a laboratory experiment, by ingesting some substance or other. What would I do? Having knowledge of this lesion, I would distance myself from it, knowing that I would not see, for example, the right side of my visual field. When I wanted to see objects located in front of me, I would turn my head and eyes, thereby reconstituting a new complete field by means of a praxis that would in a sense render the deficit inoperational.

A real hemianopic, in contrast, whose lesion is the result of a physiological process, is unaware of his deficit; and he maintains the unity of his practical field of vision. The two things go hand in hand: he does not say that he has lost half of his visual field, only that he sees a little less well, that it makes him a little more tired. The optical system is complete to the extent that it has reconstructed itself: all the points on the retina have moved, because they were unable to go on organising vision around the central point, with a lateral degradation of visibility. The reorganised centre is now located to one side and new zones of degradation are becoming established, so that every point on the retina has taken on a new function. Around the macula, where vision was formerly at its clearest, it has become most degraded; not only the retina but also focusing, muscular activity and the visual field have been transformed, so that a lateral point, where sight is usually less clear, has now become the central point. If we ask this hemianopic to identify the object in front of him, he will indicate an object located in front of this new central point, since it is around this point that the visual field is now organised.

We note that ignorance is crucial to the hemianopic's behaviour; he does what he does only because he does not understand the situation. This alteration, which happens suddenly and without his knowledge, offers us a better understanding of what subjectivity is. First, we grasp that we can apprehend subjectivity only using objective elements, which seem to us either to go beyond normal adaptation or to fall short of it. In reality, we understand that something has happened to the hemianopic – whom we then recognise as such – only once he has told us what is in front of him. This is the objective, practical structure of subjective reality. We then understand that the patient is not a person affected only by his lesion, but a being who has reorganised a totality in three parts: the organic behind him, the field of visibility without blemish or loss within him, and the object that he must see before him in order to pick it up, feed himself, live and so on. He must also experience his lacuna in interiority.

Praxis, non-knowledge and being

But what is the difference between the patient and the man we imagined, who afflicted himself with semi-blindness as a laboratory experiment? This man sets in train a *praxis*; he distances himself from the lacuna and leaves it to its inertia. He declares: 'It's something that is only an external object, which is of course involved in my act of sight, but falls into exteriority because it is merely a strict passivity.' Indeed what could be more passive than a lacuna, less active in the real sense of the word? At the same time he accommodates, copes, turns his head to right and left and ultimately does what he wants. He has a *praxis* based on theoretical knowledge. What about the other man, the true hemianopic? He also transforms his visual field, but because he is unaware of his lacuna he integrates it. Having been only external, it becomes totally internal. It has been adopted from inside and can be regarded as directing the entire reorganisation of behaviour, as a practical organiser. This thing, this material lacuna, is suddenly integrated into behaviour as a result of non-knowledge, because it is experienced without distance, and behaviour embodies the adoption without distance of something that belongs to exteriority. There is undoubtedly negation here, but it leads to integration. It is no longer the complete negation of a distancing *praxis*, but a negation that is integration in ignorance. It is a blind negation of the deficit, which establishes that deficit at the centre of the new organic life. This blind negation is not accompanied by any recognition of lacunary being and, in denying it, integrates it into the whole.

In other words, whatever happens, the whole remains and changes while claiming not to have changed, because it does not know the change. The patient is not hemianopic because he is deprived of half of his visual field – that would amount to regarding this state as a passive disturbance, when it never remains passive. He is hemianopic because he makes himself so, because he maintains a totalisation from within by integrating the deficit. This is the first essential characteristic of subjectivity: if subjectivity is, by definition, non-knowledge, even at the level of consciousness, it is because the individual – the organism – has to *be* his being – *être son être*. This is possible in two ways: one consists in being one's material being, as in the case of a pure material system – here the deficit exists and that is all; the other consists in altering the whole through practice in order to remain what one is, even if it means accepting certain alterations – this is the more complex case of *praxis*. But between the state of inertia of a system and *praxis* proper, there is the condition of interiority, which means that the whole does not exist as an initial given, which then has to be maintained, but is something that must be perpetually maintained, which must always-already be maintained. There is no given in an organism; there is a constant drive, in other words a tendency that is one with the construction of the whole. And this whole that is being built is immediately present to each part, not in the form of a simple, passive reality, but in the form of organising schemas that require – the word 'require' is purely analogical – a retotalisation of the parts in all circumstances.

We are dealing here with a being for which the definition of interiority is having-to-be its being, in the form of an immediate presence to the self, but at the same time with the slightest possible distance in the form of a regulated and self-regulated totality, which is at once present in every part and the presence of every part in each. In reality the whole is a law of interiorisation and perpetual reorganisation. In other words, the organism is first and foremost a totalisation, rather than a whole; the whole can only be a kind of self-regulation which perpetually brings with it this interiorisation as totalisation. Totalisation occurs through the integration of an outside that disturbs and changes, of which the hemianopic is an example. All in all, the whole is no different from the overall drive. The drive and need are one. We cannot say that there are needs first; there is one need, which is the organism itself as a requirement to survive. It is only afterwards that a complex dialectic with the outside, which we have not considered, leads to the specification of particular needs; at the outset the need is the maintenance of the whole.

Nevertheless, having-to-be requires that, internally, being is immediate presence, and permanently so, because it is immediate presence without distance, and subjectivity as a system of interiorisation does not involve any knowledge of itself however we consider it. You will say to me, 'But consciousness exists!' So it does; but, as we have seen, once consciousness is involved, subjectivity becomes objectivity.

Politics of 'grabuge'

The case of hemianopia involves an elementary behaviour. Let me now go a little further in showing how things develop at what is more usually thought of as the level of subjectivity, in the case of a very close friend, a past and present contributor to *Les Temps modernes* who was there at the beginning.[4] There we were, about ten of us, trying to come up with a name for the journal. As you know, the aim was to adopt a critical position

4 The evidence suggests that this was Michel Leiris.

with regard to the French bourgeoisie and the right; we were of the left on principle, allied to left-wing forces, and we examined the world from that point of view, combining action with critique, in order to help change it. We needed an appropriate name, and this friend simply suggested *Le Grabuge*. This is a familiar French word that occurs in writings from the eighteenth century and means, we could say, 'anarchic violence'. For example, if people in a café started to threaten each other, we could imagine bourgeois customers saying, 'Let's go, there's going to be *grabuge*'. It is a word that evokes violence, blood and scandal—something that suddenly disrupts order. Subjectivity was immediately apparent in my friend's suggestion and created a mismatch. Of course, we were against the bourgeois order and wanted to assist its liquidation and the establishment of a socialist order as far as we could, but 1945 was no longer the time to do it in the form of *grabuge* – which might also mean that my friend would walk naked down the Champs Élysées, certain as he was that any scandal would help to undo bourgeois consciousness.

This was the strange mismatch that I will try now to explain, to the extent that it reveals subjectivity. If we suppose that my friend is called Paul, no one who knows him and who heard what he said at the time could have failed to think, 'That's just like Paul!' In other words, we all recognised him in this simple choice of a word. Why? First, because Paul is a former surrealist. He has moved away from surrealism, but he is nostalgic for it and, consequently, he is stuck in repetition. And, as Breton used to say, the simplest surrealist act is *grabuge*. You take a revolver and shoot someone at random – the act is scandalous, but also strictly individual, as destructive of yourself as it is of the other person. The surrealists got together when they were still young and cultivated this violence, which they continued to express, notably in verbal terms through literary and artistic scandals. However, none of them ever took a revolver and shot the first person he met in the street. Most of them have retained something of this; it is constantly refashioned and repeated in new circumstances. Long after surrealism, Paul would go into bars and insult someone, preferably a man much taller and stronger than him; he would end up on the floor for this act, having received a beating which deep down he did not fear – we could almost say he had gone looking for it. This is a manifestation of repetitive behaviour, not recognised as such, in response to an earlier conditioning that has been re-interiorised. This surrealist will always be a surrealist.

No doubt you could point out that other surrealists have had very different lives. Aragon, for example, has joined the Communist Party and is undoubtedly not the man to call a new journal *Le Grabuge*, but rather *Concorde* or something like that. This is a very particular situation, which must be interpreted as such. Of course, it relates to Paul's social history, which he readily recounts, because he knows himself while also not recognising himself in his suggestion. He knows himself admirably well – indeed, he has written remarkable books about himself – yet when he said that, it did not occur to him that what he had written was coming to the surface. He was just thinking that he had chosen a good title for a journal.

Paul was and remains a petty bourgeois from a rich family, whose childhood – which it would take too long to describe – means that bourgeois life has a hold over him and suits him. He cannot really escape it; his education has given him a personal need for certain bourgeois attitudes, a certain bourgeois comfort, although at the same time he detests these things. He is in the classic position of what are called anarchists – not right-wing anarchists, because he is sincerely anti-bourgeois, but he also knows well that he is held back by a number of things. What is the action that he constantly repeats? The two aspects are inseparable. In 1920 Paul appeared at the top of the staircase in the Closerie des Lilas café in Montparnasse and cried out 'Long live Germany! Down with France!' This was definitely not a thing to shout in 1920. The people at the bottom of the stairs told him to come down, which he hastened to do, after which he spent three or four days in hospital. What was he doing? As far as he could, he destroyed bourgeois reality through scandal, and in so doing destroyed the bourgeois within himself, in an act of self-destructive, not to say suicidal violence. There is an element of that in *grabuge*.

This takes us still further into subjectivity. There was a moment, a few years after the Soviet revolution, when *grabuge* appeared to all parties on the left to be the best possible inclination for an intellectual. The bourgeoisie was very strong, the USSR was a newborn threatened on all sides, and both the Communists and later Trotsky himself were saying, for exactly the same reasons, 'Your role as intellectuals is to destroy the bourgeoisie, to destroy it as an ideology. You are ideologues, so steal its words, provoke it with scandals!' This attitude indisputably had tactical value in its day, around 1925–30, but it no longer has any meaning when the social problem and the international problem are posed in new terms. These days, analysis, study and discussion are more important than pure scandal in combating bourgeois forms of domination. But Paul has maintained a certain past, and it was this that led to his mismatched suggestion.

It was not only his own bourgeois reality, but the preservation of a tactic that had been valid in 1925, is no longer so today, and which he has not left behind; he is still attached to it, and that is where subjectivity lies. Moreover, he did not simply suggest one title among others; he suggested it as something that would commit us. I cannot imagine all the things we might have published if we had accepted it – the wildest articles on sexuality, pornography, articles advocating murder and so on – because the choice of a title like that would have signified that we did indeed want to perpetrate. This indicates that the exteriorisation of subjectivity implies something like giving it institutional form. If we had accepted Paul's suggestion, his own person would have become, through that title, our shared obligation. It is quite a striking case: either Paul's suggestion was adopted, and his subjectivity became a set of duties, or it was rejected, and this same subjectivity slipped into oblivion. As things turned out, we did not adopt it, because we knew what we were doing.

Let us imagine, however, that we had been looking uncertainly for something else. We could have sealed the journal's fate by giving it a totally inappropriate title. It would be impossible for us now to publish, as we do, stories about torture in Algeria, for example, if we bore the name *Grabuge*. We would seem to be presenting such things to scandalise our readers, when we are presenting them so that all of this can be properly dealt with, so bringing the war in Algeria to an end. Conversely, advocates of *grabuge* cannot but rejoice at this war. In reality, Paul himself has gone beyond that: he is as hostile to the Algerian war in his actions as it is possible to be. But it remains the case that back then he projected himself and proposed that title because he was being the self he was and did not know. These are distinct moments. If, after the event, we had told him what his suggestion meant, he would no doubt have accepted what we said, but at the time he put forward objective arguments: 'It will be more attractive to the public, it will express the negative side, and so forth.' He certainly did not say, 'I like it, and it's what I want'. He did not say it because he did not know it.

Repetition and inventiveness

This example offers us an opportunity to observe two traits describing subjectivity proper. For human beings there are several dimensions to subjectivity – subjectivity itself being ultimately their totalisation. First there is what is current, *actuel*. I would say, for example, that Paul's class being has remained current, insofar as his class being, which is a particular way of rejecting the bourgeoisie while being unable to separate himself from it, is a constitutive element of his being that is not of the order of the past, but timeless; it truly is his class being, in other words, the form of his insertion into the bourgeoisie. On the other hand, his relationship to Surrealism is a relationship to the past because, after all, if he had not been involved in the Surrealist movement, if he had not at one time participated in a project that allowed him to satisfy his appetite for *grabuge*, he would not have felt it. So there are two dimensions of subjectivity that must be perpetually re-totalised, without their being known: the past and, at the same time, class being. We have to be our class being, we are not it. We have to be it, in the sense that we are it only in the form of perpetually deciding, subjectively, to be it.

At the same time, we have to be our past. To regard the past as a set of memories that it is always possible to evoke is to reduce it to something passive, a set of objects that are available to us and which we can line up before us. To this extent, the past is already no longer me; it is a quasi-me. But, for this past to exist all the time as the possibility of distancing oneself from it, it must be perpetually re-totalised. This implies that repetition is a constant in subjectivity. Because we endlessly re-totalise ourselves, we endlessly repeat ourselves. Paul never stopped repeating himself in this way, from the moment he cried 'Long live Germany!' at the Closerie des Lilas to the moment he suggested *Grabuge*, and indeed long after, in different circumstances. His past is there in its entirety, but in the mode of non-knowledge, non-consciousness, in the form of a necessary re-integration, and this past in turn is linked in a contradictory way to his class being. While his class being may lead him to be something else in different circumstances, the past, on the contrary, implies repetition.

Subjectivity appears as both repetitive being and inventive being. These two characteristics are inseparable, because Paul repeats himself in circumstances that are always new, and always projects the same being through inventiveness, in circumstances that are quite different. Because it is inventive to get yourself beaten up in the 1920s by shouting 'Long live Germany!' and it is also inventive to suggest calling the journal *Grabuge*. It is an adapted response –although the adaptation is not always successful – to new circumstances with a new inventiveness. The raw material, as it were, of the inventiveness is subjectivity itself. We will never recognise and understand what human inventiveness is if we assume it to be pure *praxis*, grounded in clear consciousness. Elements of ignorance are necessary to permit inventiveness. So we can say that subjectivity has two characteristics that are essential and contradictory. Through them human beings repeat themselves indefinitely, although they never stop innovating and, by this very fact, inventing themselves, since what they have invented reacts on themselves. *Grabuge* is at once repetition and inventiveness.

Inkblots

There is a third essential characteristic, however. This repetition-innovation within a particular, immediate relation, always transcendent to external being, is called projection. This means that what is essential in subjectivity is knowing oneself only outside, in one's own inventiveness, and never inside. If subjectivity knows itself inside, it is dead; knowing itself outside it does indeed become an object, but an object in its results, and this leads us back to a subjectivity that is not really objectifiable.

Projective tests have meaning only if we assume that we constantly project ourselves into the object. A projective test is an answer to a question posed by an experimenter and the subject depicts himself totally in the answer or set of answers. But how could there be particular questions that lead the subject to depict himself entirely, if he did not depict himself entirely constantly and everywhere? We cannot think that the projective test is an exceptional situation. The clearest case is the Rorschach test, which consists of images showing shapes and colours with no definite structure, because it is for those who take the tests to provide a structure. In my own case, I saw absolutely obvious things in a Rorschach test but, as soon as they were compared to other interpretations, the objective perception of something obvious suddenly became weak and schematic – which is a curious experience that anyone can have in other circumstances but which is a constant in this case. The perception was the projection of my own personality, without my knowing what it meant, moreover; but where I saw genial human figures, another person saw cabbage leaves. Well, I realised that in fact you could see cabbage leaves. At once my brilliant characters, whom I still saw, became simply the impoverished outline of something in me. Which shows that subjectivity must be understood as perpetual projection, and to the extent that it is a mediation it can only be the projection of being within – *en deça* – onto being beyond.

This allows us to understand how subjectivity is indispensable to dialectical knowledge of the social. It is because there are only people – there are no great collective forms, as Durkheim and others imagined; and these people are obliged to be the mediation between themselves of forms of exteriority such as, for example, class being. As we said earlier, at every moment these people create a singularisation of class being, which is thus a singular universal, or a universal singularisation. In these conditions, it is at once something transformed by history and a structure that is indispensable to history because, at this level, we are no longer dealing with a being 'below', *en deçà*, as we were before. We are already at the more complex level of what, in *Critique of Dialectical Reason*, I called the practico-inert, in other words a quasi-totality in which matter always prevails over the person, insofar as it is itself mediation.

The being of a worker in a factory where there are automated machines, for example, is defined in advance. It exists, it is a particular place, not in the form of pure inertia, not in the form of the requirement of a being, but in the form of an inert requirement of the machine. Let us take a factory which, in the context of capitalism, is obliged to produce a particular amount to generate a particular profit. According to a particular norm, it uses a particular machine, which implies a particular human function and a particular wage. Supposing that the capitalist's profit will be as high as possible, and that the machine is newly bought, a being is thus defined who is undoubtedly not yet current and, with her, the wage, the type of work – including the type of work-related illness – and, through her, an entire family. As I wrote in the *Critique*, a worker is defined not only by the type of inner reverie that the machine obliges her to have, but also by her pay, her illnesses, the number of children she has and so on.[5] Certainly, along with exhausting work and pay, it

5 *Critique of Dialectical Reason, Vol. I: Theory of Practical Ensembles*, London: NLB, 1976, pp. 232ff.

allows her the possibility of having just so many children and not one more, unless she is to give them up to the social services. While all this is imposed in the manner of inert requirements, a world nevertheless begins to take shape in which people can struggle, come into conflict, deceive and dominate one another as soon as subjectivity has to take that turn – *a être cela.* The concrete social reality is not the machine but the person working at the machine, who is paid, gets married, has children and so on. In other words, worker or bourgeois, one has to be one's social being and one has to be it in a way that is first and foremost subjective. This means that class consciousness is not a primitive given – far from it – and that, at the same time, one has to be it in the very conditions of work.

Subjectivity of skill

In another passage of the *Critique*, I cited an example to which, in concluding, I return, in order to show what I mean by this. Around 1880, one type of worker was defined in the clearest possible way by the universal lathe. This was a qualified worker who had done two years' apprenticeship, took pride in his work and was surrounded by unskilled labourers. The machine defined him because once there is a universal machine,[6] one that is not closely connected to particular functions and performs perfectly only if it is supervised, you need a man who can do that work, a trained technician. That is the first thing. You also define a certain number of beings around this qualified worker – men, or rather 'sub-men', unskilled workers who are denied any kind

6 'This means a machine – like the lathe in the second half of the nineteenth century – whose function remains indeterminate (in contrast to the specialized machines of automation and semi-automation), and which can do very different jobs provided it is guided, prepared and supervised by a skilful, expert worker', *Critique of Dialectical Reason*, p. 239.

of qualification and are simply there to give him a tool, take the waste to the other end of the factory and so on.

From here, a certain type of social being had been created which had to be realised. It would be realised by the skilled worker, and that meant that subjectively he would accord particular value to his work. In place of a class struggle founded on the need that inspires 'a humanism of need, as the direct hold of every man on all men',[7] as happens today, there was a time when value was conferred by work – real, intelligent, skilful work. In fact, in France at that time there were anarcho-syndicalist writings that seemed to say that it was less unjust to pay unskilled workers poverty wages than to pay skilled workers badly—in which they failed to grasp the problem of surplus-value. Above all—and rightly, moreover—they regarded themselves as the very foundation of society, seeing that they worked and made objects that others used, and were badly paid even though they did the most valuable work. They shared an aristocratic idea of work. Unskilled workers were poverty-stricken and should be helped, of course, but the injustice they suffered seemed less flagrant in that they had no skills. Thus, a certain way of experiencing the situation subjectively becomes established, which could not fail to go hand in hand with a position of prestige. Such positions had immediate importance in struggle, because more often than not these skilled workers were devoted to self-education; they read a lot in that epoch, despite the long working hours; they regarded themselves as the ones who would make the revolution, giving a lead to the unskilled and educating them.

We are dealing here with a kind of worker aristocracy; around them would gravitate the people who were to be helped

7 Ibid., p. 243.

and raised up but who, for the moment, really were inferiors within the context of the working class itself. This translated into the choice of a particular form of unionisation. When the time came to raise the issue of forming industrial unions, the skilled workers opted for craft-based organisation, because that would exclude the unskilled. Objectively, this gave rise to a particular kind of union struggle that was real enough at the time, because in practice it was enough for the skilled workforce in a factory – the minority – to go on strike for operations to cease, even if the unskilled majority wanted to go on working. The union practice of the time, the kind of self-valuing, the type of struggle and form of organisation, corresponded strictly to what those workers were, to what the machine was. We are not saying here that they were wrong or right: they were all that the universal lathe allowed them to be. It was in them, as their superiority; they interiorised it, and this interiorisation, or subjectivation, produced the whole phenomenon of anarcho-syndicalism.

This was not, as Lukács claims, because they did not grasp the totality of what the working class was and what its struggle was. On the contrary, because they were at the centre of production, they did grasp it as it was at that time. It is true that at that time they were far better qualified than the rest, but it is also true that this led to the development of yellow unions, an aristocracy of labour and a host of fairly aberrant secondary elements reflecting that conception, that interiorisation in the form of social superiority, which disappeared wherever work that required training was replaced by semi-automated, then automated machines. But in that epoch they could not have been expected to foresee the existence of such machines, practically and in their struggle. Of course, Marx described them in *Capital*, but he was a theorist, a leader of the International, not a worker who struggles at every instance of his life, someone who is formed by the machine and at the same time internally transforms it. Which means that class consciousness itself has its limits, which are the limits of the situation as long as that situation has not been completely revealed.

Should this lead us to describe this type of 'class consciousness' as empty? Should we decide that the anarcho-syndicalists were not the men required? On the contrary, it is because they were aware of their strength, their courage and their worth, because they established unions and specific forms of struggle, that other forms of struggle could emerge in the era when specialised workers appeared. In the course of struggle, the subjective moment, as a way of being inside the objective moment, is absolutely indispensable to the dialectical development of social life and the historical process.[8]

Translated by Trista Selous

8 Trista Selous translated this lecture from Italian into French for publication by Editions les Prairies Ordinaires; this English rendering is based on that French translation.

DISCUSSION WITH JEAN-PAUL SARTRE

With the interventions of Mario Alicata, Bianchi Bandinelli, Galvano della Volpe, Renato Gattuso, Cesare Luporini, Guido Piovene, Lucio Lombardo Radice, Giuseppe Semerari and Francesco Valentini

Subjectivity and Knowledge

Summary of Lucio Lombardo Radice's[1] intervention

Lombardo Radice argued that there is, indeed, an objective dialectic, which is not limited to the dialectic of nature alone. That does not, however, justify the dogmatic Marxism that claims to be able to enumerate the general laws of the dialectic. He emphasised that there is a dual crisis: the crisis of subjectivism, which marks the end of anthropomorphism in science – as even some representatives of subjectivism itself, such as Heisenberg, have pointed out; but also the crisis of objectivism. In his presentation Sartre specified that the subject's self-knowledge implies a destruction or modification of the subject; but that is also true of knowledge operating at the microscopic level of 'electrons, quanta, and very small particles'. And so Lombardo Radice asks: what role does the subject's creative activity play in the knowledge of those natural phenomena that are not at the level of human sensibility? – hence questioning the validity of objectivism and of knowledge-as-reflection. Finally, Lombardo Radice commented that knowledge of oneself can very well be projected outside of the self, and then become a process of a collective character that does not entail the destruction of the subject.

---

1 Lucio Lombardo Radice (1916–1982), a mathematician and member of the Italian Communist Party's central committee.

SARTRE: First, I think that a misunderstanding may have arisen from the way in which I posed this question. The problem in question was subjectivity, and indeed I spoke of subjectivity. But I do not see how reality can relate to neither subjectivism nor objectivism. I am entirely working on the basis that the two notions – of subject and object – are senseless when taken in separation from one another. There is a Hegel text that is very clear on this point, where he says that the trouble with the expression 'subject-object relation' is that even when we speak of a *relation* between subject and object, 'subject' and 'object' take on meanings that they do not hold in common, and they instead tend towards isolation.[2] So when you speak of subjectivism, I think that you are referring to a theory that has, in any case, never been my own. In truth, the question that interested me – and afterwards we will have all our discussions – was that, given that there is reality, and

2 'Consciousness, we find, *distinguishes* from itself something, to which at the same time it *relates* itself; or, to use the current expression, there is something *for* consciousness; and the determinate form of this process of relating, or of there being something for a consciousness, is knowledge. But from this being for another we distinguish being in itself or *per se;* what is related to knowledge is likewise distinguished from it, and posited as also existing outside this relation; the aspect of being *per se* or in itself is called Truth . . . But the nature of the object which we are examining surmounts this separation, or semblance of separation, and presupposition. Consciousness furnishes its own criterion in itself, and the inquiry will thereby be a comparison of itself with its own self; for the distinction, just made, falls inside itself. In consciousness there is one element *for* an other, or, in general, consciousness implicates the specific character of the moment of knowledge. At the same time this "other" is to consciousness not merely *for it,* but also outside this relation, or has a being in itself, i.e. there is the moment of truth. Thus in what consciousness inside itself declares to be the essence or truth we have the standard which itself sets up, and by which we are to measure its knowledge'. G.W.F. Hegel, *The Phenomenology of Mind*, Introduction, §§82, 84, text taken from www.marxists.org/reference/archive/hegel/works/ph/phintro.htm.

sectors of interiority within it, which we are (if you like, there are beings, organisms, which we are, and there are other realities that are inorganic beings, which we are not), in what measure is the passage to objective knowledge achieved by way of subjectivity? And subjectivity, moreover, is simply our proper being, that is, the obligation on us to have to be our being, and not simply passively to be. So from this point of view, I think that there is a very serious discussion that must be had, but it will certainly not bear on the cases where we would say, like some of the scholars whom you cite: 'man knows only himself'. You referred to Heisenberg,[3] but Eddington[4] said the same thing; and all this represents an idealism that I believe has today been completely transcended. The true problem is, in fact, that of knowing how, through an objective knowledge of the real, we who exist subjectively can transcend ourselves in order to have a relationship with reality. That is the first problem that I wanted to pin down, and we will discuss it further, if you like; I only spoke of subjectivity when that was the matter in question.

---

3 Werner Heisenberg (1901–1976), a German physicist, who was one of the founders of quantum physics. The question of subjectivism and its here-announced crisis crystallises around the famous principle of incertitude, or indeterminacy, according to which – to stick to a formulation given above – we cannot know simultaneously both the speed and the position of the electron around the nucleus, and this is not because of any imprecision in the measurements themselves. Heisenberg drew an anti-objectivist and anti-determinist lesson from this: 'Natural science always presupposes man, and we must become aware of the fact that, as Bohr has expressed it, we are not only spectators but also always participants on the stage of life': see his 'The Representation of Nature in Contemporary Physics', reproduced in *Symbolism in Religion and Literature*, ed. Rollo May, New York: G. Braziller, 1960, p. 221.

4 Arthur Eddington (1882–1944), English astrophysicist, author of *The Nature of the Physical World* (1928).

Then you say: to know oneself is to destroy oneself; I did not say that, I said that to know oneself is to change oneself, and most importantly, it is to pass from one status to another. To you that seems astonishing, and you asked me if I wasn't myself fundamentally the victim of my own subjectivity; well, I'll agree on that much, precisely to the extent that I consider that we are all, from this point of view, subjectivities transcending ourselves towards the object. But I must remind you that what I said, most importantly, is that there is a change in status. The examples of scientific knowledge that you give can be summarised by Louis de Broglie's line, according to which the experimenter is part of the experiment, and, as a consequence, for a certain number of scholars – I don't know what you think; you're more qualified than me to say – but for a certain number of scholars, doing an experiment in microphysics is already to change the thing – for example, in adding some particles of energy. So we certainly agree, at that level – but that does not mean changing its status; here, we are changing it practically, but we are changing it just like how I can change the place of this microphone, or we give it an energy it had not had, or we are incapable of calculating simultaneously both its speed and its position, in the same measure that we cannot say that we are doing anything with our movements other than intervening as a physical force in a physical world, or, if you like, as a material force in a material world.

On the contrary, when it comes to knowing ourselves, I did not at all say that we always in practice manage to change ourselves; far from it, since the anti-Semite who knows himself to be anti-Semitic will very often remain anti-Semitic. I said that we change in status, that is, that we pass from subjectivity to objectivity, and that the relation that we have with ourselves is changed. You will tell me, I know very well that I am not anti-Semitic; I am sure of it, too: I am not anti-Semitic, I am not racist. But you know no better than I do if you totally aren't. Only through experience will you learn if your anti-racism is not a particular species of honest, violent reaction against racist tendencies that you still have, or if it truly means a complete absence of racism. It would be to believe in the purity of a drop of water (and again, not the scientific drop of water, but of the drop of water viewed as such) to imagine that we have a knowledge of ourselves that allows us to say in an absolutely rigorous fashion: 'I am not racist.' What we can say is, 'I will make every effort to erase any racism within me. I will make every effort to fight the racism inside of me and outside of me.' But it's happened to more than one person – like, for example, the worker I spoke to you about this morning, who doesn't believe himself to be anti-Semitic – that they suddenly discovered by chance that they were racist. And I could tell you stories of people in France who didn't believe themselves to be anti-Semitic, and became so at a moment during certain episodes or affairs. They came to see that they were anti-Semitic, having believed that they were not.

But we ought to be very attentive to the fact that that is not at all what subjectivity is: at first it is not, 'we are nothing', and then, thanks to some complex situation that we reflect on, we see that we transcend, interiorise and objectivate it; at that moment we see the reality of what we are, which often surprises us, and the fact of knowing this reality sets us in a different relation with ourselves. Here I am alluding, for example, to analysis. Analysis, psychoanalysis, is a method often employed by charlatans, and its underlying metaphysics isn't a good one. But as a technique for putting oneself in perspective by relation to an onlooker, there is something truly excellent about it, in the sense that it is a moment where we open up our thinking about what we are, and we see things that we did not know. Not because they were so sombre and horrible that we had neither the courage nor the will to know them, but simply because our mode of being means that we live what we are without such distance, in a state of absolute presence, and we discover what we are only by way of objects to which we refer in order to know ourselves. As a consequence, we absolutely must not think that we are returning to some mysterious foundation; this is not at all a matter of declaring that there is I-don't-know-what deep and hidden source of existence. As we rightly said this morning, citing Marx, man cannot but be a natural being, he is also social, because he then distinguishes himself from nature, but if you try again to go beyond that, you have nothing. So there is no question of seeking some deep origin, an existence under the opening to being, as in Heidegger. There is nothing of the sort. This is just man, and simply man. The manner in which he is present to himself, at first, excludes knowledge.

Then there's the last point that I would like to discuss. You say that the case of the hemianopic is of no great interest to you. But the hemianopic is the anti-Semite who does not know that he is anti-Semitic, or the honest man who becomes anti-Semitic even though he knows that he is not racist, because there is some political circumstance whereby the Jewish elements of a society suddenly become politically troubling for that society. At that moment, they are brought together and reconstituted as a totality that very much entails anti-Semitism, in a different form. It is impossible, as concerns our own fifty-six years of history – and maybe for you it will be more or less than for us – but it is impossible for us to say after the fact that we were clear *a priori* and to say that we really know that we are this or that thing. We know nothing at all. What we can try and do is to be clearer, by constantly exercising an objectivising control on ourselves. But it is utterly impossible to determine exactly what we are unless we have the proper circumstances to reveal it to us.

Again, on that last point, to which I would like to return, it seems to me that you are addressing a problem that does not come under the remit of what we decided that we would be talking about here – even though it is a very interesting question, which I discussed with my French Communist friends when I was up there a few days ago – namely, the problem of the dialectics of nature. I would just like to remark that here you are introducing a little subjectivity when you present the dialectics of nature as a certainty, though you only provide us with other certainties, scientific considerations – and that is not entirely the same thing. For example, if the theory of evolution were complete, if it were fully formed, then it would probably be a dialectical theory. I say 'probably' because it could be otherwise, given that we know just one thing, namely that there is evolution, but at the present moment – with the crisis of biological thinking – it is impossible to specify the manner in which this evolution has taken place, without this being a subjective choice. At this moment there is no coherent, proven theory of evolution. There is an irreducible, real fact, that there is evolution. We did not appear without there having been earlier links in the chain, among the first forms of the individual; but that is all that we can say. In the same manner, when you consider science today, it is true that the subjectivists are, fortunately, losing ground, but it is also true that this is taking place within the context of a considerable crisis of science. And, to get back to a very interesting aspect of what you said, this crisis itself comes from the limits – be they definitive or temporary – of our knowledge as limited organic beings; or, as many physicists think, it could perhaps simply come from the fact that the mathematical material that would allow us to deal with certain problems has not yet been produced. But, in any case, this crisis does not allow us to consider the dialectics of nature as anything other than something that you don't like, that is, fundamentally, an anthropomorphic projection. There is a clear, intelligible dialectic in historical materialism. That is to say, I can understand not only the objective fact and the dialectical real, as you explained it to me, but also the dialectic itself, to the extent that it functions therein; I understand the dialectic starting from the totalisation that is history. So there, I understand the negative, the negation of the negation becoming affirmation, starting from the whole. After all, I can clearly see how in a whole, an isolation – which is a negation – can be suppressed through a fact that follows it, and we return to a positivity of the whole; to a superior differentiation, for example. There I understand what is taking place, internally to the whole that is the historical whole. Starting from the moment that I declare that the ensemble of physical-chemical knowledges today, for example, which are effectively knowledges in progress, in enormous progress, but which, precisely because they are in progress, are in crisis – so, starting from the moment that I declare that these knowledges are of a dialectical order, at that very moment I transpose what I know into the human order. Because as you say, this is the very crucible of Marxism: it is man, man in historical materialism, man defining himself within a society through his acts and through his objective reality as social man. So, then, that is a thought that is valuable for man. And I'll pose the following question, entirely outside of our remit today: don't you think that there's a degree of anthropomorphism, in projecting this in time? I do not deny the possibility of a dialectic of nature; I say that it would be a different one. Here we have a difficulty.

Those are all the responses that I wanted to give.

On the Dialectic

VALENTINI:[1] I want to venture a few remarks on your [Sartre's] presentation this morning. I would kindly ask that you consider my observations as a series of questions, and not as objections.

You spoke of subjectivity, and in a certain sense your presentation also related to your book *Critique of Dialectical Reason*. But I got the impression that you were sticking to the first part of this book, and in particular to the practico-inert. You cited a few examples that don't go beyond the level of what you call the practico-inert. And I would be keen to ask you whether you think that the theme of subjectivity is still useful from a research and analytical point of view, when we do go beyond the practico-inert? When you speak of the group and of history – and I'll return to the problems posed by Lombardo-Radice and by those who intervened after him – when it comes to looking at and discussing what we call history, and even when it comes to what we call nature, the subjective appears to have lost its function. So I would be keen to know whether you believe that, even at this level of research, the heuristic category of 'the subject' can still fulfil a role?

I get the impression – and in saying this I don't mean to criticise you – that your book as well as your presentation this

1 Francesco Valentini (1924–), philosophy historian, and author, in 1958, of *La filosofia francese contemporanea*. He published *Il pensiero politico contemporaneo* in 1979, and *Soluzioni hegeliane* in 2001.

morning have a Hegelian rhythm. You've presented us some examples, and Paci has told us, pretty clearly, indeed, that Robinson does not exist. That might remind us of what Hegel said, prior to the *Phenomenology of Spirit* proper, when he presented examples like those of master and slave, sensation, perception, etc. And I believe that the examples that you have given us have the same function as the dialectical figures that Hegel talked about in the first parts of *Phenomenology of Spirit*.

When Hegel spoke of the spirit as such, when he spoke of the French Revolution – analysing the Terror, which you have discussed at a number of points in your book, he was no longer speaking of subjectivity. When he gives his outline description of the Terror, he does not talk about Robespierre at all. It seems that, for Hegel, the problem of subjectivity was of no use in analysing dialectical levels, higher levels, that is, the levels that transcend what you have called individual *praxis* as well as the *praxis* of the practico-inert. The question that I would like to ask you – and I think this may also entail another question – is the following: how can you explain the relations between your position today, which you call Marxist, and the research that you undertook during what we might term the first phase of your thinking?

You offered us a brilliant theory of consciousness in your first article[2] – I think that it was your first phenomenological piece regarding your philosophical research – in which you spoke to us about transcendence and the Ego. You also spoke of

2 'La Transcendance de l'Ego: esquisse d'une description phénoménologique', *Recherches philosophiques*, no. 6, 1936/37, pp. 85–123, republished by Sylvie Le Bon under the same title in 1966 (Paris: Vrin) and then by Vincent de Coorbyter, *La Transcendance de l 'Ego et autres textes phénoménologiques* (Paris: Vrin, 2003).

the structure of consciousness in your *Being and Nothingness*, where you distinguished between consciousness, as being for oneself, and the being of things, an inert being in oneself. Many of us have read your works and studied your thinking, and we thought that we could discern a certain idealist orientation in your theory of consciousness. I believe that we can also say that these critiques felt the influence of Hegel, that is, that the mind is not only perception, that the mind is not limited to the level of perception, but that there are also higher levels where consciousness, properly speaking, has no function. At this level, Hegel himself spoke of the great man, but that's something else. That is the first question that I would like to pose to you.

I'll specify that this perhaps also concerns the same question that we might pose when we think of Hegel's assertions in his critique of the philosophy of reflection. And I, for my part, believe that existentialism – even your own, up till the most recent phase in your thought – is a philosophy of reflection; that is, that the mind is not only perception, not only consciousness. That poses what is evidently a very important problem, one that we could try and resolve (on this point, I think that we'll have the opportunity to hear from other people who are here today, who are specialists in this regard), a question that concerns the relations between your position today, your dialectical position and phenomenology in the Husserlian sense, but also in the sense that you elaborated it in your earlier works.

I will make one further remark. Today you didn't talk about a category which is – I believe – central to your *Critique of Dialectical Reason*, namely the category of scarcity, which you have elsewhere spoken about a number of times: you have even said that man is the historical product of scarcity. I believe that our thinking can draw great benefit from what you have said elsewhere. For example, the formula in *Being and Nothingness* that 'Man is a useless passion';[3] or 'man is an absolute',[4] as you put it in your Presentation of *Les Temps modernes* journal, if I am not mistaken; or lastly, 'Man is a historical product', that is to say, the product of scarcity. In this sense, it is evident that knowledge is not a pure consciousness, but it is itself historic, having undergone the effect of scarcity. If that is true at the elementary level, for example at the level of the individual and of the practico-inert, I believe that it is all the more true at higher levels.

---

3 'Every human reality is a passion in that it projects losing itself so as to found being and by the same stroke to constitute the In-itself which escapes contingency by being its own foundation, the *Ens causa sui*, which religions call God. Thus the passion of man is the reverse of that of Christ, for man loses himself as man in order that God may be born. But the idea of God is contradictory and we lose ourselves in vain. Man is a useless passion': *Being and Nothingness*, p. 615.

4 'No, a worker cannot live like a bourgeois. In today's social organisation he is forced to undergo to the limit his condition as a wage-labourer. No escape is possible; there is no recourse against it. But man does not exit in the same way that a tree or a pebble does: he must *make himself* a worker. Though he is completely conditioned by his class, his salary, the nature of his work, conditioned even in his feelings and his thoughts, it is nevertheless up to him to decide on the meaning of his condition and that of his comrades. It is up to him, freely, to give the proletariat a future of constant humiliation or one of conquest and triumph, depending on whether he chooses to be resigned or a revolutionary. And this is the choice for which he is responsible. He is not at all free to choose: he is implicated, forced to wager; abstention is also a choice. But he is free to choose at the same time his destiny, the destiny of all men, and the value to be attributed to humanity. Thus does he choose himself simultaneously as a worker and a man, while at the same time conferring a meaning upon the proletariat. Such is man as we conceive him: integral man. Totally committed and totally free. And yet it is the free man who must be *delivered*, by enlarging his possibilities of choice. In certain situations there is room for only two alternatives, one of which is death. It is necessary to proceed in such a way that man, in every circumstance, can choose life': Jean-Paul Sartre, 'Introducing *Les Temps modernes*', in *'What Is Literature?' and Other Essays*, Cambridge, MA: Harvard University Press, 1988, p. 265. Translation altered.

Last question: this morning you cited a number of examples of dialectics, and Lombardo-Radice and Luporini have also continued citing them. You drew these examples above all from biology, ones related to biology, and you presented examples of dialectics. I remember that there was the example of hemianopia, that is, pathological damage to the vision. You also spoke of the organism – that is, of the totality that is, in sum, the organism. Your dialectic is above all this dialectic of totality; in this sense, it is Hegelian. I think that Della Volpe is completely right on this point: here we are dealing with the dialectic of totality, of the Hegelian totality. But for me that – perhaps it is not worth saying, but it is best to say it anyway – is not a criticism that I am directing against you. I repeat: I only want to pose you some questions.

We could take a lot of examples from the level of biology and biological research, where there is this structure, this configuration, that is totality. In his book *Phenomenology of Perception* [1945] Merleau-Ponty also elaborated at great length on examples where there was every sign of this dialectical structure and of totality. I remember his famous example of the amputee and his phantom arm, in which the amputee tries to reconstitute this totality.[5]

I would like to pose the same question to Luporini, by referring, in a certain sense, to what Colletti said:[6] do you believe that there is something fruitful to be gained, at this level, from talking about dialectics and totality? For my part, I thought of the judgment-through-reflection in Kant, that is to say, the teleological judgement that does not add any new knowledge, and

5 *Phenomenology of Perception*, trans. Colin Smith, London: Routledge & Kegan Paul, 1962, pp. 76ff.

6 Valentini is referring to a prior intervention by Lucio Colletti, not included here.

which is nothing but a kind of ideal and method for the scholar, but is not properly speaking a synthesis but only a reflection, a judgement. However, the true judgement that provides a new knowledge is not that one; it is a determining judgement. I think that we could cite numerous examples even in the biological sciences, within which the structure of totality does have its proper function. For example, when Luporini spoke of a real contradiction, I thought of the contradictions, so to speak, among the vegetative, sympathetic and parasympathetic nervous systems, which all have an antagonistic function and all represent, so to speak, a contradiction in reality. But I ask myself: is this a true contradiction? Is there some use, something fruitful to be drawn from emphasising that? I think that it adds nothing, from the point of view of adding new knowledge.

I will moreover refer to what Luporini spoke about: the question of the unification of the sciences and the function of the dialectic. Personally, I think that the dialectic is a question that concerns the spirit – meaning, the Hegelian spirit. For example, I'll mention that Father Fessard, who is a dialectician and a Hegelian, has mounted a very interesting study of St Ignatius's spiritual exercises, basing himself on the Hegelian dialectic. That works very well.

That is not a criticism, but I believe that there do exist experiences – that is, what we call the experiences of the spirit (master and slave, and also the spiritual exercises of St Ignatius, which Father Fessard spoke about)[7] – in which the schema of the dialectic proves its fruitfulness. However, I would struggle to believe that

7 Gaston Fessard (1897–1978), Jesuit. The work here being referred to is *La dialectique des exercices spirituels de Saint Ignace de Loyola* (Paris: Aubier, 1956). This was the first volume out of three: the second was issued in 1964, and the third in 1984, by the same publisher.

this schema also has this same fruitfulness when it comes to historical research; that is, I think that it is above all an anthropological question, expressing a certain anthropomorphism.

We can say that, if the Hegelian dialectic does not always operate, then it is not a law. Indeed, I don't think that it is a law. In my view, it is a monist prejudice to believe that there is any one law under which all phenomena could be brought together. These are monist prejudices. There are no laws, there exists no law, as general as that. I believe that reality is much richer than that. If we thought that such a law could exist – claiming that there is this dialectic that can be found as a fundamental structure everywhere – then whoever replied that there are many more things in the world than our philosophy can even dream of would always be in the right.

SARTRE: I am going to reply to your points in reverse order – that is, starting from your last question, which moreover seems to me by far the most interesting and generally important one, because fundamentally it poses the very problem of the dialectic, and also extends some way beyond the question that we have come here to discuss. I should start by outlining the extent to which I am in agreement with you, since I do think that the projection of dialectical interpretations onto nature – when the scholar is not resorting to it as a method – has the status of a working hypothesis, or of a regulating principle, or of a Kantian idea, and I am not against that. It is for scholars to see whether that bears them some fruit; I will simply note that, in fact, scholars today do not make much use of it. The scholar, as a scholar, does not use the dialectic a lot, and I would even add that when we envisage these antagonistic forces not on the plane of positive and negative, but truly as an orientation in the universe, that still does not give us a dialectic. It simply gives us directions, orientations, or even oppositions, but not contradictions. So, you'll find that I agree with you entirely, with regard to the limitations of the dialectic. That's where the problem gets more difficult, it seems to me: when it comes to asking whether within history itself, at the level of historical materialism, we have some dialectical segments and others that are not – as you seem to indicate – or if we have to imagine it as an entirely dialectical ensemble. And I would like to reply on that point. I do not at all consider the dialectic either as a law or as a set of laws. We can devote ourselves to making laws, on the basis of dialectical movement; perhaps we can produce a logic of the dialectic – Lefebvre did. Why not? But that seems to me wholly secondary.

The true problem is to know whether history is a totalisation or not, and, if it is a totalisation, knowing what are the structures of a real ensemble that totalises itself. That is the level at which I speak of the dialectic. For me, the dialectic is simply that. It is not totality, but the ensemble of structures of a totalisation in process. And when I tried to write a critical work on the dialectic, I did so precisely because it seemed to me that in all the literature – not only the Marxist literature, but all the literature, because everyone is talking about dialectics – the dialectical fact was completely obscured; we don't understand anything about it anymore. I also cited a quite unbelievable text of Lévi-Strauss's in which he speaks of the dialectic as a dichotomy. Yet a dichotomy is anything but dialectical, since what it does is separate out its elements. So what I tried to do – and I believe that it's one of the things that we can try to do – was to render some intelligibility to the dialectic; not a Hegelian intelligibility, not one that starts out from the self-forming Spirit, but a material intelligibility at the level where men are among themselves and where there is totalisation. So, if you will, the problem that needs discussing is a dual one; and if we did discuss it, then the question would be: is totalisation a fact in human society? I think that Marx himself responded to this when he said that production is a whole; that the production process is a whole. There you have it. Effectively, there he gave an answer. And why is the production process a whole? That takes us back to the biological individual, or rather, to the psychosomatic individual, because man, need-work-pleasure [*besoin-travail-jouissance*] is himself a whole. It is on that basis that the relations among men, in a binary form, in the form of asymmetrical or symmetrical relations, ordered by relations with nature, etc., can begin to constitute a totalisation, and it is starting from this totalisation that we can try to know – not *a priori*, but in history itself – the conditions for the loss of a totalisation. So it's there that we have to find an intelligibility of the dialectic, because we are ourselves the beings who make the dialectic; it is not an individual fact, if you will, but an inter-subjective fact, a human fact. That is how I'd respond to your question.

As for the examples I used that are of a psychosomatic order, I used these – like that of the hemianopic – because they go beyond a simple organic reaction; because I think that we cannot truly establish a dialectic based on the organism, and we remain outside of it in order to observe its phenomena of self-regulation, synthesis, etc. But from the moment that there is a psycho-somatic being like man, and once the elements of perception, reflection, knowledge and ignorance, and conduct are involved, then we have a totalisation. And that is what is happening in the case of the hemianopic, because this is not a matter of a non-human organism, in which we could observe more or less tendencies for the whole to maintain itself, as, for example, if we removed a frog's brain. In reality this is the question of a man, integral in his personhood, who on account of facts that are not only somatic but also psychic, tries to recompose this whole that is heading towards disintegration. That is why I took this example, because it also plays out on a level that I would call the material plane, in the sense that here it is not a question of ideas or ideation or objectivation – here, we are on the plane of simple perception. And in perception we can see this attempt at retotalisation, which can give us the primary laws of the dialectic.

And in this respect, I will reply in particular to a criticism that you made of me, when you said that you hardly see why there should be an opposition, a contradiction, within a whole, a totalisation. I will reply by bringing you back to your own critique: I do not understand how there could be contradiction in an infinite nature. I cannot conceive of contradiction except within a unity where two opposed forces, whether they are conscious or not – that is of no importance – either destroy the unity or entirely take it over. I can understand the class struggle within a totalising society, within a unity like French or Italian society. I cannot understand the struggle or contradictory antagonism of two forces that belong to a universe made up of shattered fragments that surround us and are fixed around a particle. Here, we do not have the idea that the unity will be remade on the basis of the destruction of one of the two forces – as in the case of the destruction of the bourgeoisie by the proletariat – or on the basis of the other force – the bourgeois class, which presents itself as the universal class guaranteeing this unity. Here, we do not have the fact of each of the two being the bearer of the whole, and that is what is very important here. So that is my reply to your first question – fundamentally, I consider the materialist dialectic as the only way of envisaging the development of history. I see no other way, and when I tried to write a book on the materialist dialectic I did not do so in order to change it, but to try and see how we could free it of a too-common usage and restore its clarity, which is fundamentally translucency – not an always-given translucency, but a postulated translucency of man with man.

You asked me why I did not address the question of scarcity in this regard. But that was because, if you will, fundamentally the subject is insufficiently defined. For my part, I wanted only to indicate the extent to which subjectivity makes itself in creating objectivity. There is a reality: this reality is a field of interiorisation or an exterior field, and there is a synthetic relation between the two. I do not believe that there is any possibility of creating an objective without this objective being precisely a reality's seizing-in-interiority of the ensemble of being; and this reality makes itself subjective in creating, capturing or discovering – as you will – the objective; the objective being simply the matter in front of this reality, insofar as it has a relation to it. And I had no need to place myself within the historical perspective of scarcity in order to indicate that. It would be different if you now asked me how this subjectivity is conditioned, how man – on the most indirect plane furthest from scarcity, as well as on the plane closest to it – is conditioned, how his subjectivity itself is entirely scarcity, how it is even scarcity itself that makes the individual's activity. By that I mean that, when certain conditions create a society in which a man is necessary – not because it needs him, but because there are forces that are mutually paralysed and as such there needs to be a symbol, etc. – this man is himself a scarcity, since he either will or will not be found, and if he is found, he will never be the man that the situation would imply; and as such, we have a singularity in the situation that comes precisely from his scarcity.

So I'll gladly let you have all that. It's just that I did not want to address this perspective of a historical order, because for me the true problem is the following: what exactly is the synthetic object–subject relation? And you ask me then, to what extent will subjectivity intervene in the historical forms that transcend the practico-inert – that is, if we follow the hypothesis that there is a transcendence of this practico-inert, which is itself necessarily objective-subjective, and is an inert requirement, because there are men behind it who have real needs; it is men as inert requirement, it creates a system. So I will answer you first by saying that the total dissolution of the practico-inert is not a given, it is not ours. It is a problem that is posed even in a socialist country – the practico-inert does exist there – because it can be produced not only by oppression, but simply by the relation between man and machine, the demands that the machine and the economy place on man, that are retransmitted, etc. There is a practico-inert everywhere, and consequently there is, at this level, a subjectivity everywhere. But also, most importantly, in the socialist countries there is a group effort to break out of that. So at that level, we get to what I just told you, and I think that this is the important thing – that the class or the group or the party is all the more the agent of history the more that it is its own object. To put that another way, subjectivity does persist, but on the one hand it endures as a reality that is weakened in reflection and, on the other hand, it is an object that is at each instant malleable. That is one of its characteristics that we do not emphasise enough. There is a French historian, a right-wing one indeed, who has emphasised this in his analysis of the changing attitude towards the body, birth, death and the family over the last century. This historian, Philippe Ariès, wrote a work entitled *Attitudes devant la vie et devant la mort du XVIIe au XIXe siècle, quelques aspects de leurs variations* [1949], noting the extremely interesting fact that everything that was subjective with an ideology of the natural in the eighteenth century – for example, with regard to the birth rate – in the nineteenth century instead became a person's operation on her own body, with all the bourgeois practices of birth control. In the eighteenth century, they had children without any birth control and relied on death to take them away, so they did arrive at a certain equilibrium; but this balance was constituted by a sort of *laisser-faire*. Children were born, they died; and they let one and the other thing happen. But in the nineteenth century, conversely, with all the bourgeois practices of birth control, the person captured her own body as an object, including in the domain of sexuality. Similarly, our own attitude towards death and the body to be cared for is entirely new: that is, a body is now for us simultaneously both the subjectivity that we are and the object that we are. We see this very clearly – for example, when we look at the difference between a man trying to climb the Annapurna massif fifty years ago and a man trying to do so today. Today this man treats himself as an object, he uses every opportunity to increase his capacities and his strengths, so he has nothing in common with the man who tried to do the climb in previous eras, and who was only an agent, but an agent overwhelmed by his own subjectivity. So we can say that starting from the moment that a group or a class really, truly becomes conscious of what it is, and at the same time, becomes class-conscious – for that is the same thing – it becomes conscious of itself as an object in order to be able to act, in taking account of its objective limits and in utilising them. Like the phrase – I am not sure that Lukács said it, but it more or less corresponds to his line of thinking – that the more you are an object for-yourself, the more you are a subject.

But the problem that you pose has a certain resonance – perhaps Piovene will talk more about it in a moment – that echoes the problem of art, on this level. If we imagined a society freed of subjectivity, not because subjectivity no longer existed, but because it was always kept in the state of an object, then could we conceive of an artist in such a domain – and what is the role of subjectivity in art? This is a whole other problem. At this level, you are right, then, to say that what I tried to do was at the level of what we call a philosophy of reflection. This is not a philosophy of reflection in the sense of the mind reflecting on itself, but a philosophy at the level where there is a distance to oneself – really created by reflection: a philosophy trying to define the social person and the group in its objectivity, starting from subjectivity. You saw today, for example, how I tried to describe a character to you, on the basis of what he had spoken about – '*le grabuge*'– and you see that this was not truly a matter of reflection in the ordinary sense of the word. After all, reflection in the ordinary sense of the word would not need to convey the whole of the person's life starting from that basis. Rather, it was an analytical regression, which should, then, push towards a synthetic progression; and in what I say later I will describe this progression, how we pass to history, and, specifically, the role of subjectivity. So I think that's the answer that I should give.

LUPORINI:[8] If I understand you correctly, I think that you have posed a rather polemical question. That is, you presuppose the existence of a moment of transcendence in which subjectivity persists only in a state of objectivity. What decides that? Is that what's at issue? Is that quite right? So I think that I'll have to

8 Cesare Luporini (1909–1993) taught the history of philosophy at the Universities of Cagliari, Pisa and Florence until 1984. Having initially been of an existentialist bent, he then turned to Marxism and was a member of the PCI from 1943 until 1991. He was an elected senator from 1958 to 1963 in the third legislature of the Italian Republic. He opposed the transformation of the PCI into the PDS (Partito Democratico della Sinistra) and instead sided with Rifondazione Comunista. His Marxism was founded on a critique of historicism, rejecting economistic Marxist dogmatism. Among his most important works was *Dialettica e materialismo* (1974).

reject this question, as a matter of principle – in the sense that I think that there will never be such a moment, when subjectivity is maintained in social life only in a state of objectivity.

SARTRE: No, that's not quite right. I said that reflected subjectivity – the subjectivity that is the object of reflection, if you will – would be maintained in the state of an object; but reflection itself is, in substance, subjectivity. Or an immediate, unreflected consciousness. We have seen how the fact of its existing without distance makes it subjective, but in certain cases of contradiction, as in, for example, the case of the worker who is simultaneously both Communist and anti-Semitic, there is cause for the emergence of a reflection that grasps this first consciousness, this first subjectivity, as a reflected subjectivity; it grasps it almost as if at a distance. It is this first consciousness, the consciousness that is reflected, that I think will be more and more objectified in the sense that we can increasingly grasp it in its objective motivations, like those men and women who are very much involved in their own psychoanalysis, and at the very moment that they see certain movements of anger, fear or anxiety arising within themselves, manage to grasp them in an objective form. Which does not prevent subjectivity from appearing, since in any case man is subjectivity, and cannot be anything else. That is all that I wanted to say, and there can be no question of eliminating subjectivity from nature.

Marxism and Existentialism

SEMERARI:[1] I get the feeling that in general this debate has not sufficiently taken into account the presupposition at the basis of the *Critique of Dialectical Reason*. Probably Sartre himself, in his summary exposition of his position, did not do enough to emphasise this assumption. At bottom, the *Critique of Dialectical Reason* emerged at a particular moment: it had precedents that we can find even within Sartre's own works, as well as in the cultural and political situation of our time. Everyone knows that the core around which he built the *Critique of Dialectical Reason* was the very long article 'Search for a Method' [otherwise known as 'The Problem of Method', first published in *Les Temps modernes* in 1957.[2] And 1957 is a date

1 Giuseppe Semerari (1922–1996), specialist in contemporary philosophy from Husserl to Lukács, professor of philosophy at the University of Bari, director of *Paradigmi*, a journal of philosophical criticism. His many works include *La filosofia come relazione* (1961) and, with regard to Sartre, Vito Carofiglio and Giuseppe Semerari, eds, *Jean-Paul Sartre: teoria, scrittura, impegno*, Bari: Edizoni dal Sud, 1985.

2 '"The Problem of Method" was an occasional piece – hence its somewhat hybrid character, and the fact that it seems to approach problems somewhat indirectly. A Polish journal decided to devote its Winter 1957 issue to French culture, intending to give its readers a panorama of what we still refer to as "*nos familles d'esprit*". Many different writers were invited to participate, and I was asked to write on "The situation of Existentialsm in 1957". . . . My article was subsequently republished in the review *Les Temps modernes*, but I altered it considerably to suit French readers. It is this version which is published here. The title has been changed from "Existentialisme et Marxisme" to "Questions de méthode" ("The Problem of Method"). Finally, my

of some significance, when it comes to our reflections on this question. This came just after the Twentieth Congress [of the Communist Party of the Soviet Union] and the [1956] events in Hungary. Sartre had already published *Being and Nothingness* [in 1943] some years previously. Between *Being and Nothingness* and the *Critique of Dialectical Reason* there were works like *L'Humanisme littéraire*,[3] *Adventures of the Dialectic* [1955] and even Merleau-Ponty's *Phenomenology of Perception* [1945]. Merleau-Ponty is not discussed in *Critique of Dialectical Reason*, but I think that he is very much present in this work. That is not to deny the originality and novelty of Sartre's method and the coherence of the method that he deployed in *Critique of Dialectical Reason*, with respect to his previous works.

But this morning I would like very briefly to draw the attention of all our friends in attendance to the question that is at the very beginning of Sartre's *Critique of Dialectical Reason* – that is, to draw your attention to the introduction. Throughout what I say, here I am taking the position of a disinterested onlooker – relatively disinterested from the viewpoint of Marxist orthodoxy, as well as from a non-Marxist point of view. That is, the position of someone addressing the problem of the goal that Sartre set himself when he wrote the *Critique of Dialectical Reason*.

We find a formulation of this problem right at the start of the book. Sartre says: My goal is to pose the problem of our time, which interests us as philosophers, politicians, sociologists, ideologues and psychologists, as men of culture

---

intention is to raise one question, and only one: do we now possess the materials for constituting a structural, historical anthropology?' *Critique of Dialectical Reason*, pp. 821–2.

3 An apparent conflation of *Existentialism Is a Humanism* (1946) and *What Is Literature?* (1947).

and also as common men, the problem of how we can construct an anthropology, that is, of a radically, integrally human conception of man. In order to arrive at such a vision, in order to enrich this perspective of a theoretical character – and it is, after all, a theoretical way of looking at things – we need to decide on certain steps and to make certain cultural choices.

Now, Marxism makes up part of our field of choices as a possible operational tool in putting together this structural and historical anthropology. In my view, this is a fundamental point. But when I was listening to the various interventions yesterday, I got the impression that this perspective was being somewhat sidelined, and that fundamentally we were discussing the alternative between a sort of absolute choice, or else a Marxism that wholly inserts itself within contemporary culture and yet does not recoil at the possibility of being radically revised.

Yesterday we heard the intervention of an illustrious colleague who disagreed, and who said, 'Of course, we could do that, but if we did, we would have to be careful, because we would be putting everything into question'. And that is precisely the point: we have to be ready to discuss everything, as appropriate, as necessary. But, I thought, the problem lies somewhere else. The decisive choice is between a Marxism that presents itself as open to and prepared for even the most radical revision within the context of contemporary culture, and a Marxism closed in on itself, which becomes scholastic, and, even if it declares itself open to dialogue, nonetheless closes in on itself again as soon as dialogue starts to produce its effects – thus becoming, in a certain sense, a formula that is the answer to everything.

Besides, we know of earlier analogous cases in the history of Western culture. For example, at the level of Christianity, which has undergone fundamentally the same process. In certain aspects, Christianity has become a formula that claims to be able to contain all the cultural possibilities of our world, and all the more so in that it declares itself ready to accept determinate forms of post-Christian culture.

And following the various interventions of our Marxist and communist friends yesterday, I noted that this concern was very much present – the concern that the dialogue between Marxism and currents of non-Marxist origins could transform into a process of revising Marxism, into a radical questioning of certain fundamentals of Marxism, and especially when the debate brought into relief the points of contact or derivation between Marxism and Leninism. If we put Hegelianism into question, then Marx's fidelity to Hegel becomes a fundamental question. If we outline the limits to Hegelianism, then we must also outline the limits to Marxism, and vice versa.

But it seems to me that the way in which Sartre posed the problem is aimed, on the one hand, at freeing Marxism of the pre-Marxist elements that continue to operate within it, and, on the other hand, at proposing an interpretation of Marxism that brings Marxism itself back to its original core, which we'll term 'existential' in the broad sense, to use Sartre's language. As a result, after 'Search for a Method' came out, Sartre's work was interpreted as an eclectic attempt to fuse existentialism and Marxism. It has been said that the existentialism that became susceptible to Marxism at a certain moment is the existentialism that finally learned Lukács's lesson on existentialism-Marxism and began to situate itself on the terrain of Marxism. It has been said that the *Critique of Dialectical Reason*, read literally, would itself ultimately authorise such an interpretation. Indeed, Sartre is explicit, categorical: he defines existentialism as a parasitical philosophy, a philosophy that lives on the margins of the philosophy of our time, namely Marxism.

However, at a certain moment Sartre attracts our attention to the fact that even though existentialism can and must be considered a philosophy that parasites on Marxism, it also has its own necessity and its own reason to make itself felt within Marxism: the need for existentialism within the dimension of Marxism itself, by which we mean existentialism's own existential project. So the attentive reader will not have failed to note – on page 125 of the *Critique*, I think[4] –Sartre's statement according to which, as soon as Marxism accepts the existential method and makes it its own, that is to say, the method of the existential project, it will no longer be right to speak of existentialism and Marxism as just so many antagonistic and unilateral positions. On the contrary, existentialism will concretely have realised philosophy in the world, philosophy in its mundane becoming and, ultimately, the essential philosophical problem of Marxism itself.

If, initially, it may have seemed that Sartre had converted to Marxism, a more attentive reading suggests that this was more a question of an 'existentialisation' of Marxism, which implies, therefore, a profound transformation of the structures and categories of such an existentialism or such an interpretation of existentialism.

Now, when I refer to these motivations or these elements that contributed to the introduction to the *Critique of Dialectical Reason*, my intention is not that this will be of solely philological value, but rather that it is fundamentally important for

---

4 Semerari is clearly citing the 1960 French edition. To see the basis for the argument he is here elaborating, it is worth looking at the whole first part of the introduction (pp. 115–35 in the 1960 edition, pp. 135–59 in the 1985 one) rather than just the page cited here.

appreciating the *Critique of Dialectical Reason*, its relation with Marxism, and Marxism itself, within their historical context and in a radically historical manner.

Today it is no longer possible to address the question of Marxism invoking only Marx's own texts, that is, the texts written by a man who lived from 1818 to 1883. I remember hearing a number of interventions yesterday in which the speakers were keen to emphasise that Marx himself had recognised the existentialist foundation of *praxis*, in his *Deutsche Ideologie* and his *Thesen über Feuerbach*. In the *Deutsche Ideologie* he clearly says that the presupposition of the historical process is constituted by really existing individuals, individuals acting concretely.[5]

Some people have pointed out that the problematic of sensibility is present in the *Theses on Feuerbach*, in the *1844 Manuscripts*, and later in *Capital*, etc. They cited these references in order to emphasise that everything that was later developed in the *Critique of Dialectical Reason* already existed in Marx. In a certain sense, that is true, but in another sense that's not the case, since we have to occupy ourselves with Marxism today, in 1961, in the middle of the twentieth century; and twentieth-century Marxism can no longer be considered independently of its Leninist and Stalinist developments. This, too, is Marxism.

If we were to situate ourselves on the terrain of debating Marx's texts, taken as such, then we would certainly be doing a very useful and very important job. But I am not sure that this can help us to develop the structural and historical

5 'In direct contrast to German philosophy which descends from heaven to earth, here it is a matter of ascending from earth to heaven. That is to say, not of setting out from what men say, imagine, conceive, nor from men as narrated, thought of, imagined, conceived, in order to arrive at men in the flesh; but setting out from real, active men, and on the basis of their real life-process demonstrating the development of the ideological reflexes and echoes of this life-process' (*Marx/Engels Collected Works*, vol. 5, p. 36).

anthropology that we spoke about earlier, and to define the philosophical-political work we need in order to make this anthropological project concretely realisable, and not limited to a simple rhetoric destined to run its course. In this sense, it seems to me that the discussions emerging on the political terrain, like, for example, the suspension of socialist legality[6] – an important theme of contemporary debate – must appropriately be brought to the level of the problematic that we are discussing here, in order to verify to what degree Marxism, in its ideology, contributed or did not contribute to defining these positions, which are certainly not Marxist, nor democratic, and leave us extremely perplexed as to what a generically Marxist way of posing this problem would look like.

But before concluding my intervention – which, I repeat, did not propose to offer solutions, but only to call our conference's attention back to these presuppositions, these foundations of Sartre's discourse – I would like to mention two points in the introduction to the *Critique of Dialectical Reason*, that is to say, the 'Search for a Method'.

1. Page 18, note 1:[7] Sartre establishes a relation between Hegel, Kierkegaard and Marx, and recalls – using the language

6 Here Semerari refers to Khrushchev's 25 February 1956 'Secret Speech' on 'the cult of personality and its consequences'. He said that the expression 'enemy of the people', invented by Stalin, had 'made possible the use of the cruellest repression, violating all norms of revolutionary legality, against anyone who in any way disagreed with Stalin'.

7 For the English edition, see *The Problem of Method*, London: Methuen, 1963, p. 9. Referring to Jean Hyppolite's 1955 book *Études sur Marx et Hegel*, in this note Sartre emphasises that it is possible to 'draw Hegel over to the side of existentialism', with 'his panlogicism complemented by a pantragicism'. Yet, he continues, that is not where the problem lies: what Kierkegaard opposes in Hegel is the fact that he neglected the '*unsurpassable opacity* of lived experience'. Indeed, for Kierkegaard, the man is the *signifier*, who himself produces significations, none of which target him from the outside: 'he is never the *signified* (even by God)'.

of contemporary semiology – that, from Hegel's point of view, the signifier is always the Spirit, the absolute Spirit, absolute History, while the signified is the individual in his concrete aspect. Conversely, according to Dewey[8] the signifier is always and only the individual, but the individual considered in his abstract character. But, for Marx – and we are perfectly in agreement here – the signifier is always the individual as a community acting historically and as a historical *praxis*.

That is precisely the point that we want to see the debate take a closer look at – the question of how to conceive this signifier-community and render it operational. If it is not structured in a certain manner, does it not run the risk of becoming substantialised and thus superposing itself on the individual in his concrete determination? Or could it be structured in such a way that it can always maintain the freedom and openness of the communication between the individual and itself ? It is clear that Marxism would truly be in the avant-garde of modern thought if it was able to provide a positive resolution of this problem.

2. The second point, with which I will conclude my intervention – and I'll ask you to excuse me if I have gone on too long – regards what Sartre reminds us of in note 1 on pp. 30–31[9]

---

8 It would be impossible to present the *oeuvre* of John Dewey (1859–1952) in a footnote. So we will limit ourselves to saying that he was an eminent representative of pragmatic philosophy (not to be confused with pragmatism in the everyday sense), who was also an 'activist' (again to use the American vocabulary). His works include *The Public and Its Problems* (1927) and *Art as Experience* (1934).

9 For the English edition, see *The Problem of Method*, p. 32n1. This very long note is a recap of the theory of consciousness (and not theory of the subject) that Sartre had advanced in *Being and Nothingness*, on the basis of which he constructed what we might call an a-naturalist materialism in *Critique of Dialectical Reason*. To cite the first few lines: 'The *methodological* principle which holds that certitude begins with

with regard to epistemology, the epistemological interpretation that concerns the Marxist-materialist foundation of the problem of subjectivity: he brings into relief the bracketing of subjectivity between parentheses, from the Marxist and then Leninist point of view.

So even if this may seem paradoxical, he slips on the one hand towards a form that's proper to constitutive idealism, and, on the other hand, to a form that's proper to sceptical idealism. The point is this: subjectivity must be considered as immersed in a circularity, which, starting from subjectivity, results in the objectivity of the world, and vice versa. So, in this sense, subjectivity has to be considered a functional moment, as a critical-functional moment. From this point of view, it seems to me that here Marxism opens up, and decidedly so, to pragmatism in its most noble and classic form, namely Dewey's form of concrete existentialism, which I don't think we can define as a bourgeois philosophy in this regard.

So it is important to consider subjectivity as the critical moment, as the moment of critical suspension, as the moment of the reduction of the objective situation. In my very modest opinion, Marxism has bequeathed us two fundamental, absolutely positive teachings: the first is that of the human foundation of knowledge, of culture and of science; the second, the teleological perspective in which the construction of our

---

reflection in no way contradicts the *anthropological* principle which defines the concrete person by his materiality. For us, reflection is not reduced to the simple immanence of idealist subjectivism; it is a point of departure only if it throws us back immediately among things and men, in the world. The only theory of knowledge which can be valid today is one which is founded on that truth of microphysics: the experimenter is part of the experimental system. This is the only position which allows us to get rid of all idealist illusion, the only one which shows the real man in the midst of the real world'. This was a materialist perspective that he had already heralded in his 1936 *Transcendence of the Ego*.

knowledge must be inserted – a teleological perspective which, in its popular form in the 1848 *Communist Manifesto*, appears as the perspective of building a society where the freedom of each becomes the condition for the freedom of all. In Kantian terms, it can be conceived as the perspective in which man is an end for the other man. I think that we have to hold on very tight to these two points, if we want to have a discourse that is both critical and at the same time constructive, in light of the experience of twentieth-century Marxism and not that of the Marxism of the nineteenth century.

Art and Subjectivity

PIOVENE:[1] Sartre and Luporini found themselves in agreement on a point that is, certainly, general in character, but which is nonetheless a substantial one. Namely, they agree in affirming that even though it is not easy to find Marxism's sense of subjectivity, this is nonetheless something that remains at the very centre of Marxist thought. It is no appendage to it. If I am citing him correctly, Luporini said that 'the objective pole is not Marxism's only concern'. Sartre's discourse has been very productive for me, both in terms of the points of view that he proposed and the stimulating character of his intervention.

I would now like to lay emphasis on the problem of art – a question that I think is part of the problem of subjectivity. I will say it frankly: it seems to me that this problem has been neglected and very little examined in recent Marxist studies. There is no satisfactory doctrine or in-depth theory of art elaborated on the basis of Marxist precepts. This is, certainly, a lacuna, since such a theory is essential.

The fact of having a satisfactory doctrine of this kind – or not having one – is a criterion for art itself, because for a system to be able to explain and understand art is a proof of its validity and completeness. If the system is not up to the task of

1 Guido Piovene (1907–1974), writer and journalist at *Corriere della Sera* and *La Stampa*. His major works include *Lettere di una novizia* (1941) and *Viaggio in Italia* (1956).

providing one, then that reveals a lacuna, which then affects all other sectors, speaking to a true lack of in-depth analysis, and in particular with regard to the problem that we are discussing at the moment – the problem of subjectivity. To go back to what Sartre has said, I would like to start precisely with an objection, which at bottom is not truly an objection – or, if we have to say that this is an objection, then it has but one goal, which is to provoke a response on his part, or, at least, to initiate a certain order of discourse.

During his presentation, I was struck by the fact that he presented us with the example of the communist worker who feels a very strong antipathy when he is faced with a Jewish comrade. At a given moment, the worker comes to be conscious of the fact that he is anti-Semitic. This consciousness, Sartre tells us, is in itself something useful, because it helps him to transcend the contradiction that persisted within him, thus setting off a conflict between his being-communist and his being unconsciously anti-Semitic. Evidently, in order for him to be consistent, he has to eliminate the anti-Semitism that he has thus recognised.

However, then I got the feeling that Sartre does not always consider coming-to-consciousness of one's subjectivity to be a positive thing. I asked him about this in the course of a private discussion we had, and he confirmed this feeling. He told me, for example, that for certain works of art, and even for works of art in general, for the artist to be absolutely conscious of his own subjectivity can be useful, and yet this does not mean that he cannot also benefit from a certain degree of unconsciousness of his own subjectivity. And I have to say, frankly, this leaves me rather doubtful.

Indeed, he confirmed this argument yesterday in passing, when he was talking about *Madame Bovary*, and maintained that this novel simultaneously expressed both a representation of provincial France in a particular era, and Flaubert's own unconscious – in large part unconscious – projection onto Madame Bovary and that whole environment. He seemed to want to give this unconsciousness a positive value, which raised my doubts.

I would instead ask whether art has not always been a becoming-conscious of one's own subjectivity, but a becoming-conscious that reconstructs its history, the manner by which we arrive at objectivity. At a certain moment, subjectivity projects itself into objectivity, all the while maintaining a preponderant role that the artist must watch, study and constantly take consciousness of.

Let us consider the example of this now-famous unconsciously anti-Semitic worker. Suppose that this worker wrote a book, that he suddenly became an artist, and that this book was anti-Semitic in character. Would the fact that this book was unconsciously but effectively anti-Semitic diminish its value as a work of art, or not? I think that it certainly would. If that were not the case, then we would have to admit that the negativity of this book is external to art, that is, that this book could be artistically marvellous at the same time as being hateful for other reasons, from a moral point of view, in the measure that its judgements would surely earn our disapproval.

I, for my part, believe that the weakness of this book would also be an artistic one, and that this unconsciousness would also translate into artistic weakness. We cannot reply by saying that in the past there were a lot of works of art in which unconsciousness played a remarkable role, and that this unconsciousness was, in a certain sense, beneficial. But I don't know; and I'd like to leave this debate open, since by no means is this the question that we're posed.

Indeed, I think that art is today undergoing developments that are bringing it towards an ever greater degree of consciousness, to the point that the artist is ever less able to free himself of this. In this sense, I very much appreciated what Sartre told us when he said that subjectivity is increasingly absorbed by objectivity, without this however eliminating it. The development of art and of subjectivity tends towards an ever-more pronounced absorption by objectivity, whereby subjectivity changes in nature, in state, without at all being diminished or destroyed.

It seems to me that, so far as the artist is concerned, this marks an ever more clearly asserted demand for truth and an ever more pronounced refusal of any form of unconsciousness. For me, objectivation – what we call objectivation in art – preserves and even validates subjectivity: objectivity is truly something that provides foundations for subjectivity and which, therefore, validates it, in providing it with new value. For me, art is a subjectivity that knows itself and constantly inserts itself into objectivity.

Sartre addressed other points, too. He told us that subjectivity can be transcended by the response that we give to a determinate situation, and I think that this is also correct. Subjectivity is, indeed, transcended in the response that we give to a determinate situation; but in the case of a work of art, art is not only the response that we give, but also the history of our response, and, consequently, subjectivity plays a preponderant role therein. In a certain sense, I would say that the plant is pulled up together with all its roots.

I found the concept of totalisation very interesting, and in particular that of continuous retotalisation, which is a very fertile concept, because totalisation, retotalisation, is the artist's continuous movement. In art, we feel that expression must be total and that all that exists in reality must be expressed: all that exists in reality must not be denied, but, on the contrary, be expressed. Then, he very clearly brought to light the continuous movement between subjectivity and objectivity, this movement that I think every artist must know. The prolonged debate – particularly in the field of journalism – with regard to the distinction between inner man and social man is a theme that we have to move away from: subjectivity projects itself into social man and sociality is interiorised within subjectivity, in a continuous movement. I would go so far as to say that a pure and abstract subjectivity does not exist, and could not exist. I would like to hear about the experiences of each and every artist: I have one here in front of me,[2] and I hope we will hear from him after me.

I ask myself if, for example, our Gattuso has ever in his life painted a picture for the sake of the picture itself: no one has ever painted a picture for the sake of the picture itself, and no one has ever written a line for the sake of the line itself.

We all sense that in the practice of a work of art, at the most subjective moment of the work of art, this subjectivity is already dialogic. We work to realise a determinate society. All our work – even the most intimate – which we call 'subjective', is social, in a certain sense. It is always a matter of the interiorisation of sociality, or indeed the socialisation of interiority. So that was what I wanted to say – those were the points that I wanted briefly to bring to light. And I would like to add a couple of words on what Luporini said yesterday. He spoke to me in private of his desire to go deeper into what he was saying to us, particularly in the sense of a theory of art. The elaboration of such a theory would be of very great importance, for

2 Piovene is here addressing Renato Gattuso, who speaks next.

the reasons that I have presented. I strongly hope that he goes ahead with this.

SARTRE: I am rather embarrassed to respond. I share your opinion, on the points that you have presented here. I would simply like to take this as a pretext to go back and delve deeper into the idea of subjectivity. You said that sociality deeply penetrates subjectivity and that an abstract subjectivity would be meaningless; that it could not exist. I am wholly of the same opinion as you. In the sense that, for me, subjectivity is interiorisation and retotalisation, that is to say, fundamentally (and here I'll again use rather vaguer and, at the same time, more familiar terms): you live; subjectivity is to live your own being, and to live what you are in a society – because we know no other state of man, he is precisely a social being, a social being who, at the same time, lives the whole of society from his own point of view. I think that any individual, or any group, or any ensemble, is an incarnation of the total society, since they have to live what they are. Moreover, it is only because we can conceive the dialectical play of an enveloping totalisation – that is, a condensing totalisation, which I call incarnation – that each individual is, in a certain manner, the total representation of her epoch; it is only for this reason that we can conceive a true social dialectic. In these conditions, then, I think that this social subjectivity is the very definition of subjectivity. Subjectivity at the social level is a social subjectivity.

What does this mean? It means that everything that makes an individual, all her projections, her acts, and also everything to which she is subject, only reflects – but not in a certain Marxist tradition's scholastic sense of the word 'reflect' – only incarnates, if you prefer, the society itself. That is how Flaubert wrote *Madame Bovary*! What did he do? On the one hand, he wanted to give an objective description of a certain environment, the world of the French countryside around 1850, with its transformations, the appearance of the doctor replacing the health officer, the rise of a nonbeliever petty bourgeoisie, etc. He wanted to describe all these things, of which he was fully conscious. But at the same time, what was the man who wrote that, himself? Nothing other than the incarnation of all these things. In reality, he was himself the son of a doctor, the son of a doctor who had come from the countryside; he himself lived in the countryside, in Croissé, which is far outside Rouen; he had links to landed interests; he did not concern himself with investing in industry as did many people at the time . . . he was exactly what he was describing. He even went further, because to the extent that he was a *rentier*, a victim of his family, remaining in his family, dominated first by his father and then by his mother in a situation very much resembling that of the women of the time, he projected his own being onto his book's heroine. To put it another way, this book has two structures, ultimately referring back to one same one, since you can only totalise the social being that you are, and, at the same time, you describe the society that you see. The particularly interesting thing in Flaubert's case is not some extraordinary or uncommon sensibility of his – transformed by his vices or by a particularly sinister childhood – but a real life of the epoch, which projects itself, in a subjective form, into a book that claims to describe the epoch objectively. And it is precisely this contradiction and, at the same time, this overdetermination, that constitutes the beauty of his work, because instead of only dealing with people outside of him, there is a whole interiorisation of Flaubert himself, which we can feel from the outset and which we then go on to discover. The story of *Madame Bovary* is a curious one, and that is why I take it into consideration, in the sense that in

1850 this was considered *the* book – the 'Cromwell', if you will – of realism. Flaubert was *the* realist. Well, we know that, in reality, he was not a realist. He chose this subject in order to bring out aspects of himself that he had been unable to give account of in *The Temptation of Saint Anthony*, and so he wanted to situate this story in a real world, but with a whole crowd of things that were part of him. His readers little by little came to learn that this supposedly realist book in fact had two dimensions. So the first was a true, real description of a small provincial town in France, and the second was the description of a man, a more or less conscious description, projected into this first description. We learned that bit by bit – we knew it – and that is why I am going to return for a little to the question of knowing and not-knowing. We learned that Flaubert was perfectly conscious of this, saying 'Madame Bovary, c'est moi'; so he knew very well what he was doing.

The only thing is – and this is not to disagree with you; but I do want to complete my thinking with regard to what you said – Flaubert knew what he was doing, but he did not know it at the moment when he was writing. He knew it when he reflected on what he was doing, but he had never thought 'I am going to depict myself in Madame Bovary'. If he had said that, then he would have given a bad depiction of himself. I think that this was, rather, a subsequent reflection – whether he did it during his work writing the book, but at moments when he was reflecting on his work, or else afterward, since the comment comes after the book. But, in any case, it is very clear that he never had the deliberate intention of depicting himself in Madame Bovary. What he wanted to do was simply to depict a certain number of ideas that he had, which had not been synthesised properly in *The Temptation of Saint Anthony*, and which he took up in another form. So here we have three things – and it's this, I think, that makes for a true novel: an objective depiction; the same objectivity, no longer as depiction but relived in a subjectivity that projects itself, thus constituting this work as well as an identity of subjective and objective, in the sense that both relate to the same thing: the development of France in a certain era. An epoch captured simultaneously in the eyes of the now-departing health officer Charles Bovary, or those of Monsieur Homais, and also by way of Flaubert himself, feeling conflicts within himself that he projects onto it. Take the example of his hatred for Homais – which is hatred for his own father, whom he loved too much and who pushed him away; a hatred for science that is also a love for science; a very complicated mix that *is* Flaubert. So he presents Homais, Bovary, the priest, the Abbé Bournisien, etc. in an outwardly objective form, but in reality it is very impassioned. He reproaches the cleric Bournisien for not having provided him the keys to having faith – though he did want to believe – and at the same time reproaches the surgeon Homais, a degraded image of his own father, for having only poor scientific knowledge that risks inhibiting mystical ecstasy but without providing any solution to it. All of this was Flaubert himself, and at the same time, it was the real situation, since this was the epoch in which there was a great swell of de-Christianisation in France, which, starting from the Jacobins, spread across the petty bourgeoisie. But this also relates back to Flaubert, producing two forms – and it is necessary that both exist. There needs to be a kind of dense obscurity [*épaisseur obscure*], which is the manner by which you understand yourself. The book has to relate back to both these things.

If I went to Patagonia on an assignment, and then I wrote a novel on the mores of the Patagonians, I would produce a relatively objective book full of information gathered during my journey. However, it would be a very bad book, unless I produced a sort of poem putting myself in the Patagonians' place. But in that case the Patagonians would disappear, and there is not in truth enough relation between the Patagonians and me such that I could project myself. If, conversely, I wrote a novel on everything around me, the novel would be myself, as a projection, and, at the same time, everything around me; besides, I am myself everything that is around me. Indeed, here we again arrive at a practical retotalisation, the same as that which we find everywhere. That is why the strictly objective novel is, in my view, a thing of no value. There has to be this kind of condensation, the author's obscurity to himself, which can go back from there to his situation, as a totalisation. Without the author's obscurity to himself, we would get a book like they often had in the socialist countries at a certain moment: a writer sets himself up in a factory for a few weeks, comes back and then recounts what happened in the factory. He does not put himself into it or project himself onto it, because he knows that he is not truly a worker – he is a socialist writer, but not a worker – and nor is he putting other people into it, since he does not know them well enough; so what we get is a bad book.

I just wanted to point to what Gide called 'the Devil's part'[3] in the book: there can be no good book without subjectivity. Evidently there needs to be a depiction of society, in the measure that man is in it – but what really expresses the situation is the fact that he is and that he is within it. In reality, this is what we all are: people who know in the same measure as we project ourselves. There is no difference between the attitude of the poet – or rather, of the novelist – and the ordinary attitude in

3 See George Strauss, *La Part du diable dans l'oeuvre d'André Gide*, Paris: Lettres Modernes, 1985 (Archives des Lettres Modernes, vol. 219, Archives André Gide no. 5).

our lives. In practice, we capture the social by projecting ourselves onto it, but, moreover, by projecting this social itself onto it, such as we retotalise it. There is this kind of permanent envelopment and incarnation, which we need to take into consideration. So, can we really govern our subjectivity? I understand that you want subjectivity to appear more and more clearly, precisely in the name of truth, as it is certain that truth is one of the elements of art. I say 'one of the elements' because this only a matter of the truth internal to aesthetic schemas, aesthetic values, and not of pure truth. Moreover, when it comes to truth, a set of statistical data and dialectical reflections on a given social environment will always contain more objective truth than does a novel on these people. And if a novel is truer, it is truer precisely to the degree that it adds subjectivity, the subjectivity of whoever is depicting this social environment, and who in depicting it puts himself into it. But if it is true that we can better know our subjectivity, that does not mean that we could define the portion of ourselves that we put into the book; rather, it means that we are ever more reflective in relation to the immediate subjectivity that we are.

As I was telling you yesterday, the worker who says, 'It's true that I am anti-Semitic' could, in his reflection, very well become complicit in this bourgeois ideology that has been inculcated into him, and it may well be that rather than saying 'this is not compatible with my activity as a militant, and so I will get rid of this anti-Semitism', he will maintain, 'I am anti-Semitic, and that's fine. It's the communists who are wrong; Jews are indeed this and that'. And, without doubt, at the moment that we produce some work, at a certain level we can increasingly see ourselves as the object of subjectivity; and if this subjectivity is necessary to the work, we find it within reflection itself. So we can clarify that much, but then this subjectivity resumes on other terrains; even if we know it as an object, we find it again in an unknown, unseen form, because it is in the very principle of acting [*agissante*] subjectivity that it is unknown and unseen; and in the measure that the artist is projecting, he does not know himself, even if otherwise he does know himself very well. When Flaubert was writing his book, he was thinking about Madame Bovary, and when he ascribed her a certain number of reactions, he thought that these were the reactions that this woman would have; and then afterwards, reflecting on what he had written, it occurred to him that he would have had the same reactions – that he had ascribed his own reactions to her. So here, we again find the interplay that we mentioned earlier, and I think that it is impossible to conceive of art if not as the point where the subjective and the objective meet. That is more or less what I wanted to say in response, but I don't think that we are very much in disagreement on that point.

A VOICE: It is not out of some prior volition; it is a consciousness that we grasp during the work itself.

SARTRE: Yes, during the work, all of a sudden, that's it.

A VOICE: If you'll allow me, there is perhaps another thing to look into here: the life of the provincial town, of Flaubert, his father, his brother, the college, the doctor, etc. We might say that this is within Flaubert, as something that he preserves within himself, in its obscurity and in the denseness of its obscurity. So we have the proof that the thing that we call the unconscious is the exterior that is to be found within myself. Do you agree?

SARTRE: Exactly. That is what I wanted to say. It is the exterior: it is society itself. I think the society by recognising it outside of me, and I project myself, that is, I project it onto itself. At bottom, if you will, here are two different levels that are bound up with one another, two socialities; and it is the same sociality, it is the same conditioning.

A VOICE: The important thing is that we can work on that basis, analysing the word 'unconscious' in a different form.

SARTRE: I said not-knowing, in general, of reality.

A VOICE: Yes, yes, rightly so, but it's the reality of the objectivity that I preserve within me, it's not something intelligible: that is the point. Don't you agree?

SARTRE: I entirely agree.

ALICATA:[4] I agree on the fact that art does not exist without this subjectivity-objectivity relation. I believe that this is nothing foreign to Marxism. But I would like to make a small objection, in order to advance the discussion a little: does this relation also apply to poetic discourse? And how does it apply to historical discourse? I think that yesterday we even went so far as to say that this subjectivity-objectivity relation also applies, to a certain extent, to scientific discourse. That said, we have not yet defined what poetic discourse is – when, in a

4 Mario Alicata (1918–66) was an important leader of the PCI, having joined the clandestine Communist Party in 1940, the same year that he defended his thesis *Vincenzo Gravina e l'estetica del primo Settecento*. He participated in the anti-fascist resistance in Rome and worked as a literary critic and journalist; as a Party leader he was very attentive to cultural questions. A complete bibliography of his writings from 1937 to 1966 appears in R. Martinelli and R. Maini, eds, *Intellettuali e azione politica*, Roma: Riuniti, 1976, pp. 463–503.

determinate subjectivity-objectivity relation, we can say: here, we have a poetic discourse. In sum, I think that we have made only the first step. But in what manner is this problem realised? Is this subjectivity-objectivity relation characteristic of art?

BANDINELLI: Do you have something to say?

SARTRE: No, but I think that does have to be the object of the question.

A VOICE (PACI?): Allow me to speak from my point of view. I understand what you [addressing himself to an interlocutor elsewhere in the room] mean. If this schema, or this *praxis* of interiorisation and exteriorisation applies to no matter what field, that is because at a certain moment it applies either as an aesthetic, or pictorial, or musical expression, which, from this point of view, gives it its specificity. But this is a discourse that neither you nor I would grasp in the same way as a Crocean, for example, who would attribute art a determinate form of space. That is not to say that Croce[5] is not important, but a solution thus conceived is too easy.

To arrive at a more profound answer, we have to pose the problem of my incarnation, of the image, of meaning and of matter – isn't that the case? I can interiorise a social world that is also a historical world; the past, my history and the history of the world where I live. But in the externalisation, when I express

5 Benedetto Croce (1866–1952), Italian critic, philosopher and historian, and a fundamental reference point for twentieth-century Italian intellectuals. We can hardly present his thought in a footnote, but we shall highlight the fact that he professed an intransigent historicism from an idealist viewpoint. His numerous works include *Aesthetic* (1902), *Logic as the Science of the Pure Concept* (1908) and *History as the Story of Liberty* (1938).

it in not doing all the other things that are not art, I am doing a very specific work: one that first and foremost concerns language, already-constituted language – or the already-constituted language of the arts – as well as my contact with the material. So if we are talking about a painter, then this comes from his feeling for his material, and also of his degradation into material, since he himself becomes colour. In his example, Sartre spoke of Flaubert, but he pointed out that Flaubert's style also flows from that. You did not say that, but that's how it is.

There is also a reason why Flaubert was a writer and not a politician: he could express himself, externalise himself, only as a writer. At a certain moment, he said: 'I have plenty of things to do other than loving myself more than my father and my brother'. His father was a doctor, his brother the ideal son who studied at the same college as his father had. So at a certain moment came Flaubert's rebellion against his family, which was also his rebellion against this petty bourgeoisie that had made him and which he preserved within himself. From a genetic point of view, we see that in him, this rebellion expressed itself in literature, and not by other means. So this rebellion had to converge with the language of the era, the writing style of the era, and also Flaubert's own singular manner of writing.

SARTRE: It is like someone who rebels against activity. Not all artists are the same, fortunately, but that was true in his case . . .

A VOICE: Absolutely.

SARTRE: . . . and he claimed that by writing he was producing science. He said 'I have a surgeon's view'; but in reality what we have in Flaubert is literature against science. There is no doubt – it's against a certain method of science, his father's.

A VOICE: That is related to his epoch and his society.

SARTRE: He chose that it should be like that. To repeat, that is not always the case, but that is what he did.

A VOICE: I'll conclude. Alicata, in an analysis of this kind the problem that you pose does exist, but I think that it is extremely difficult. Rather than pick out the subjectivity-objectivity relation in art, in science, in morality, etc., as you said, what we need to do is take the road that explains the universality of the singular incarnation, through a regressive method.

SARTRE: There are some ordinary books that portray this fiction, and socialist books of a particular aesthetic value; in Poland, for example, books were written to describe the whole 1945–52 period after the fact, but, at the same time, they were also justifications of the authors themselves. I am particularly thinking of *La Défense de Grenade* [1956] by [Kazimierz] Brandys [1916–2000]. He is an extremely curious figure, because in a certain sense he was fully attached to the regime, such as it was at the time, and his novels were narrowly realist, socialist books in which he did not portray himself. He then started to follow another tendency: he passed judgement on himself. But at the same time as he passed judgement on himself, he did not want to disavow himself entirely. He wanted to show the errors and the failures, and simultaneously to maintain a sort of link, a continuity in conflict with change, saying, 'Ah, well, yes, there were errors, it wasn't possible to do any differently'. And he recounted this objectively. Again, take *The Mother of Kings* [1957], a novel in which he objectively recounted this period. But at the same time as he recounted it objectively, it is also clear that he himself is the hero; and that's the same thing, isn't it? At the level of a single writer, we see a development and an attempt at justification, self-critique and justification, but without his character ever appearing; and, at the same time, we see a set of characters who are captured objectively, and in whom we see this ensemble of errors, necessity and good will; derailed good will. Which means that here we are dealing with what I would call a socialist post-realist type of novel, in the sense that there is a lot more in it than the simple description of a society. It is not like when Balzac talked about the French Revolution, which was not his own work and which he only knew by way of the documents. [Brandys] is a man who truly did this, and recounts what people did. Yes, he is still recounting it with the objective methods of the socialist-realist novel, but at the same time he depicts himself within it. Which means that there is a subtlety to his analyses – and that relates to him wanting to show that he was wrong in being right; he wants to produce an auto-critique, but nonetheless this auto-critique does not 'liquidate' him as a character. Taking that as its basis, this is a remarkable novel; the author penetrates all the more deeply into the consciousness of his characters because he is himself one of them – isn't that the case? Anyway, this is something very important; it is a fact that none of us, for example, could write a true story of the life of a Pole or a Russian between 1945 and 1952. They had an extraordinary experience, this construction of socialism with all its deviations, its errors, the whole ensemble of things that went on there, and those of us who saw it only from the outside – even if we belonged to Left groups that were linked to this experience – could not describe it. It's up to them to produce today's novel. And why is it up to them? Because they were the ones who experienced it. So you see that here we find subjectivity again, in full. We can dream of sending a writer into a factory, of having him stay there for two years. But none of us would dare to write a novel on the period from 1945 to 1952 in Poland, Hungary, Russia – no one, isn't that right? – because it would have to be done by the people who experienced that. So, then, the simple fact that we recognise this proves the importance of subjectivity as retotalisation.

A VOICE: Piovene said the same thing yesterday evening . . .

PIOVENE: What I meant is that, for me, subjectivity has a preponderant role in the work of art. When you were speaking, it occurred to me that what you called obscurity-to-the-self is declining in art today, despite everything.

SARTRE: Yes.

PIOVENE: That is the point that I wanted to emphasise. This obscurity is in decline, despite everything. I believe that the artist always has more than one vision, in capturing the reasons for this vision. However, I don't think that you can be obscure to yourself at will, and I think that this element of obscurity, of productive obscurity – let's say – plays an ever smaller part.

SARTRE: The novel is invention.

A VOICE: That's it. I think that if Flaubert were writing today, he would manage to depict himself by more direct means; he would choose less long a road. I am not saying that *Madame Bovary* is not a masterpiece – clearly it is. And I'm also thinking of something else that's very important, namely that today, even in art, it is important to arrive at a correct conclusion.

SARTRE: I'm perfectly in agreement with you.

A VOICE: You can't feel that you're a liar. Probably for an artist in the past that was less important.

SARTRE: Then, too, it was very important. Flaubert's book is very true, it arrives at accurate conclusions. Thibaudet[6] has shown that Flaubert foresaw the development of the petty bourgeoisie in France, its importance to political life under the Third Republic. All that is already there in what he wrote under the Empire. But I agree with you, with the caveat that I think that in any case the subjective retotalisation does take place – at another level, but it exists even so.

A VOICE: In fact, if it did not exist, we would have no identity.

SARTRE: Or there would be a copy of yourself, an object that you would project, and that would be a bad thing.

BANDINELLI:[7] Excuse me, I do not know if it's your [Della Volpe's] turn to speak or Luporini's.

LUPORINI: I would rather speak first, for the following reason: Della Volpe has an aesthetic. I don't. It's better that whoever doesn't have one speaks first, as then we will end up with more complete answers.

---

6 Albert Thibaudet (1874–1936), *Gustave Flaubert*, 1922, revised and corrected edition 1935, now available in Gallimard's *Tel* collection.

7 Bianchi Bandinelli (1900–1975), archaeologist and art historian, specialist in classical art; a Siena aristocrat and antifascist who became a Communist after the war. His works include *Quelques jours avec Hitler et Mussolini*, Paris: Carnets-Nord, 2011, an account of Hitler's 1938 visit to Mussolini's Italy in 1938 excerpted from his *Dal diario di un borghese*, published in 1948. Bandinelli had been seconded to serve as a guide to Hitler and Mussolini during their visits to the monuments and museums of Rome and Florence.

BANDINELLI: Perfect reasoning!

LUPORINI: I asked to speak because I think that I will more be following the line of observation that Alicata indicated more than did those who've gone before me. I think that his position poses Sartre's with the greatest difficulties. I say 'difficulties' precisely because I have no aesthetic; I have problems, I have questions, perhaps because Marxism has not provided itself an orthodox aesthetic. It could be that it depends on this lack of aesthetic. In any case, I have only questions. So first I would like to pose a general problem, which concerns what I call – in translation – the 'subject forgetting itself' [*il dimenticarsi del soggetto*]. This is a fact that we always find in subjects' 'operations'. And Sartre was fully in agreement, I think, when he spoke about the man going down the stairs . . . In any operation, the subject does not think about the operation that he is accomplishing, but clearly he is thinking about the goal that he is aiming at. So the problem is to capture the subject within a determinate field: in the first place, I would say, in the field of knowledge in general. By that I mean historical knowledge, scientific knowledge and art. I believe that this element of 'dense obscurity' – this backdrop that the subject stands out from – is present in all these fields: it is present in the artist, in the scholar . . .

A VOICE: Sartre didn't say otherwise . . .

LUPORINI: . . . allow me to retrace the path that led me to these difficulties. I'm a bit of a pedant, so I have to follow a certain order. So this 'dense obscurity' is always present in operation, in the operation that is knowledge, be it scientific or historiographical. It is an artistic backdrop, which is still present in subjectivity.

For the present moment, I just want to invoke a certain experience, which isn't my own, but my wife's. I have followed it with a certain interest for a number of years. I would have preferred her to speak about it herself, but she did not want to. She worked on editing the *oeuvre* that you were all talking about yesterday evening. And editing Tolstoy's *oeuvre* means studying the process by which his novels take form, and Tolstoy's narrative form, by way of both their different variants and all that he said across the years of his work. Now, we can see that here there is a continual reflection on the self; it does not come afterward, but in the work process itself. So Tolstoy was perfectly conscious of two things: he was conscious that he was describing an objective world, and, at the same time, that he was continually describing himself. That is, he saw himself in each of his characters, not only the male ones but also in Natasha[8] etc. Which we could also prove philologically. So we could say that Tolstoy is more modern than Flaubert – and he may well also be [more modern] by the standard of a certain measure of values. But there is no doubt, thanks to philology and studies of the texts, that this consciousness is permanently present in Tolstoy – a consciousness that is simultaneously an objectivation of the two moments. I think that this objectivation helped Tolstoy: it was characteristic of him as an author and constituted the greatness of his art.

Now I get to the objection that Alicata raised: the question of art is posed starting from this point of arrival. If we agree that art is knowledge, the major problem then is to determine to what genre of knowledge art belongs. For example, if we again look to Tolstoy and this experience that I found so captivating as I followed it, then we can see that in his particular case, all of

8 Natasha Rostova, a character in *War and Peace*.

Tolstoy's characters emerged from real prototypes, from characters whom he had really met or, let's say, elements of characters that he freely mixed together. But it's not only that – that would be too elementary. Tolstoy began writing, describing and giving form to the things that interested him, by way of a style that we could characterise as naturalist, with an absolute wealth of details and supplementary aspects. The process of constituting the character consists of taking away all these minute details and creating what we could call an 'idealisation'. This is where the aesthete's discourse begins. Tolstoy was conscious of that. It was as if he were saying, 'Note: when I am writing a historical novel my goal is different to a historian's, because when I produce a description the historical character is not the same one that the historian is interested in. The historian captures the character in his historical significance, whereas I capture him in all the interlacing of real life, like other men.' So when it comes to this process of 'denaturalising' the realist prototype, could we not pose the question to which I'll return – which I'll conclude by posing, and which I do not feel up to the task of answering. For it seems to me that this is the fundamental question: to what genre of knowledge does art belong, and in what sense is it different from other genres of knowledge?

SARTRE: I will respond afterwards.

DELLA VOLPE:[9] I think the debate has arrived at a really interesting, almost dramatic point here. After Sartre's phenomenological

9 Galvano Della Volpe (1895–1968), Marxist philosopher, who had a particular interest in developing a rigorously materialist aesthetic theory. He emphasised the social production process of works of art in the formation of aesthetic judgement and emphasised the rational value of artistic creations. His works include *Critica del gusto* (1960).

description, defended by our friend Enzo Paci, we have arrived at a true question mark. True, we can grant Sartre that his phenomenological description – and I'll emphasise the word 'description' – is a very interesting one. But then we bump into the following problem: what is distinctive about the relation between subjectivity and objectivity such as it appears in a novel? What distinguishes a novel from a historical narrative?

Let's use this category of subjectivity, for a moment, and consider Mommsen's *History of Rome*.[10] This work is famous for this aspect in particular, namely the powerful character of Mommsen's subjectivity, of his political ideas. The history of Rome is analysed by way of Mommsen's own subjectivity and political perspective – the perspective outlined by his political ideas – which, we all know, led him to emphasise the figure of Caesar, etc.

So what is the difference, on this point, between Mommsen's subjectivity and Flaubert's, between the subjectivity realised in *Madame Bovary* and the one reflected in *A History of Rome*? None. What has Sartre done, in truth? Let's follow his method: with great finesse he presented us a description of the contents of *Madame Bovary*. He conveyed them to us as should be done today, namely by taking account of society, the social base. But Thibaudet had already done that. In any case, in Sartre this is much more marked. We can also do this for *Sentimental Education* [1869] and Flaubert's other masterpieces. But it still remains to be explained why this is a novel and not a historical narrative. It seems to me, therefore, that phenomenological description is a path that leads us to an impasse. But I will say that Sartre's analyses, which we get a sample of in *Critique of*

10 Theodor Mommsen (1817–1903), *A History of Rome*, Glencoe: Free Press, 1957 [1854–56].

Dialectical Reason, are very interesting – a far-reaching, brilliant effort, often even a work of genius.

A VOICE:[11] I'll specify: it is regressive and progressive, not phenomenological.

DELLA VOLPE: Certainly, it is regressive and progressive; but it is the description itself that we could term 'phenomenological'. It remains descriptive in character, and doesn't get to the fundamentals: it does not tell us what the principles of art are, and, above all, what really matters – after all, we could get by just fine without all the rest – namely what the criterion for literary criticism is, the criterion for criticism in the plastic arts and criticism in general. It's not apparent what criterion it can offer us for evaluating literary works. I repeat: the very fine analysis in Sartre's regressive and progressive description of *Madame Bovary* does not explain why these are poetic characters and not historical ones.

In my view, we have to abandon this path. Certainly, it is very interesting to note that the crisis of culture today is a very serious one. We can deduce as much from the fact that many Marxists – or many people who proclaim themselves Marxists – are interested by this form of describing art, which, truth be told, is useless because it does not show us how the historical content becomes poetry, as it does in Mayakovsky but not in other artists in Soviet Russia. That is what should interest Marxists. But Marxists have gone so far in identifying with what Plekhanov called 'the signified' – sociological values – and their attitude is so heavily determined by these abstract values, that they open their arms even to Sartre.

11 This could well be Sartre's voice; in any case, it is the voice of a convinced Sartrean.

Indeed, Sartre has already evolved a lot. What we have been presented with here is a very interesting, very instructive phenomenon. But it seems to me that – to go back to the example that I just gave – we should not follow this path, which is not worth borrowing. For a Marxist, it is a point of honour to be able to explain to a bourgeois, to a man with bourgeois tastes, why Mayakovsky is a poet, a great poet, why Brecht is a poet much greater than all those whom the bourgeois present to us as so many dramatic poets, including Pirandello. Why is Mayakovsky a poet, just like Brecht is?

The path to follow, then – and this is just my personal opinion (I am well aware that almost no one here agrees with me, but I am not too worried by that) – is a different one, which consists of seeing what the elements are that constitute the structure of the work of art. We need that in order to go beyond a vague discourse and get to the concrete: we need to start from language, and, starting from language, show how common, vernacular language acquires a power in a work of art, thus becoming poetry.

Let's take an example, which I think is a very banal, simple one, but which tells us a lot. Let's take a line from Browning, which reads 'so wore night'.[12] What tools would we need to convince ourselves, and prove to others, that not only do we feel moved by his words, but that this is poetry? In my opinion we have no other means of doing so than by starting from the text and the elements that compose it. We have to start from questions of language, and note, for example, that we cannot grasp

---

12. Robert Browning (1812–1889). The line reads: 'So wore night; the East was grey'; it is the first line of the fifth stanza of his poem 'A Serenade at the Villa' published in his 1846 collection *Men and Women*. Della Volpe inaccurately renders this phrase as 'wore the night', which he translates into Italian as *la notte si consumò* – literally, 'the night consumed itself'.

the poetic nature of 'so wore night' unless we start out from banal, common language. If we were using that language, we would express the same thing by saying 'the night passed'. To grasp 'so wore night' we have to transcend 'the night passed', which is a trivial, vulgar, unpoetic expression, but one that cannot be totally eliminated, since 'so wore night' is a metaphor. And we cannot grasp the metaphor if we don't keep in mind what is literally being signified. We find this latter in vernacular language, and not in poetry, as Croce said, following Humboldt.[13] It is a phrase in the metaphorical sense, a phrase that is a phenomenon of language and in language, in this linguistic system that has norms different from those of other linguistic systems and languages.

So how can we explain 'so wore night'? It seems to me that this is already a way of entering into Browning's verse. If I had to explain it, I would say the following: it is a metaphor, and everyone understands it as one. But the possibility of appreciating this metaphor's force of expression presupposes what is literally signified: in this case, the verb 'passes'. And even having said that much, we are only halfway. We still need to convince ourselves that there is a relation between these two elements, which could only be called dialectical.

Why is this so? Because the one cannot exist without the other: it is and it is not. We understand that 'so wore night' is poetry because it is not 'the night passed'. But conversely, we cannot explain 'so wore night' without keeping in mind the fact that these words entail 'the night passed'. 'So wore night' dialectically contains 'the night passed'. 'So wore night' shelters the literally signified, which has been overruled but is still conserved within it. I think that it is impossible to deny that.

13 The linguist Wilhelm von Humboldt (1767–1835).

And this is just a basic example, the most elementary one we could take.

We cannot grasp 'so wore night' without 'the night passed'. But it is just as true that 'so wore night' says something rather different from 'the night passed'; and yet even so, we cannot do without 'the night passed' if we are properly to grasp 'so wore night'. We cannot arrive at 'so wore night' or explain this line all by itself, with its famous synthetic immediacy, etc. It cannot be done: these are stories, myths. We cannot arrive at 'so wore night' except by starting from 'the night passed' and keeping in mind the continual, dialectical relation between the two. We are no longer dealing with Hegel's dialectic here, since the distinctions between 'passed' and 'so wore' are entirely respected. Yet at the same time the one does not exist without the other. We can only grasp that this is a metaphor by starting from a literal signified, which it deforms and confers an extension upon. The metaphor is the relation between the literal signified and the content of the metaphor. So we can demonstrate that the metaphor 'so wore night' is realised as a metaphor, and can be appreciated as a metaphor, only with reference to 'the night passed'.

The path to follow is that of analysing technique in art and in the work of art. We have to start from questions of language. I understand the comrades who are scandalised to see these questions of linguistics being posed (and that's before we even get to stylistic matters, the critique of taste); after all, these questions do not belong to our Marxist tradition. [But] we always evoke Gramsci, and, rightly or wrongly, we can also refer to him in this case. Gramsci ridiculed the famous Bertoni[14]

14 Giulio Bertoni (1878–1942), a linguist who identified with Crocean idealism and who published *Brevario di neolinguistica* in 1925 together with Matteo Giulio Bartoli (1873–1946). Bartoli had been Gramsci's professor, and his former student reproached him for this work.

precisely on account of his idealist linguistics; he wanted to unbind language[15] in order to reduce the linguistic phenomenon to the word – the famous complete, subjective, 'creative' word – when it is in fact always a phenomenon within a linguistic system.

I don't think that we can settle for what Sartre says, even if there is a great truth in his argument. It does not allow us to access the problematic specific to art, because the old categories no longer serve us here. In the example that I presented, the example of Mommsen, one of the greatest historians, we can recognise his powerful subjectivity, which indeed we find in his *History of Rome*. So the criterion of subjectivity – the traditional one as well as your own – becomes useless, because subjectivity is present in the novel as well as in the work of history.

So we have to follow another path, the path of structural analysis of the work of art. In order to do so, we have to start out from singular, concrete, technical questions, which are not in themselves poetic. Our sensibility is not used to such questions, which force us to mount an analytical effort in order to be able, perhaps, to draw out a synthesis. Of course, all that involves us being able to identify what poetry is. Starting from the example that I have given, we have to recognise what I call the 'multi-sense' [*polisenso*]: the poetic signified cannot be confused with the univocal signified of the historical narrative. The 'multi-sense' poetic signified is not the univocal signified pertaining to science, history, philosophy, etc.

I'll conclude. And I'll pose you this question: is the example that I presented – which concerned the distinction between 'the night passed' and 'so wore night', as well as the indestructible, truly dialectical relation between these two elements – only a

15 *Délier la langue*: literally it means 'loosen the tongue'.

matter of subtleties and sophisms, or is there some fundamental truth here? Does this relation between poetic and literal expression convince you? And the critic himself, when he is writing his critique – what does he have to do? Croce said that we have to start from the literal signified in order to grasp the metaphorical signified. Ultimately, that could even seem rather banal.

BANDINELLI: I'll kindly ask all those who want to intervene to pose short questions, for the moment. If necessary they can speak again. So, Gattuso, let's have your question . . . if you only put it to Della Volpe, we won't be able to hear you . . .

GATTUSO:[16] It relates to the example 'the night passed'. Indeed, the literal signified of the line saying 'so wore night' is still present in the poetic phrase; but we could equally say 'the night was destroyed' or 'the night dissolved', or something else of your choosing. The problem is the choice, all the more so since we are translating this verse from English. I would like to know why the poet made this choice, and how the critic can know that this choice was the right one?

DELLA VOLPE: The question is meaningless. The critic knows this by way of comparison. This is a continual dialectical process: by comparing what is literally given – what I call the 'literal material', in this example, 'the night passed' – with 'so wore night', we measure the gap between the expressive value of each of the two. At the same time, we cannot grasp the second without going through the first. The first is always

---

16 Renato Gattuso (1911–87) a painter, he joined the clandestine Communist Party in 1940 and participated in the antifascist Resistance. His *Crocifissione* (1940–41) is considered one of the most significant paintings of the *Novecento*.

within the second; it is a dialectical relation. We don't have one without the other; they are not each other, but we do not have the one without the other. That's the gap.

A VOICE: Excuse me – I don't know if [Della Volpe] has finished, but Sartre wants to say something right away.

SARTRE: Yes, because I am very troubled by what Della Volpe is saying, since that would make poetry the metaphorical poetry that Delille[17] was doing in the eighteenth century: the work of a poet who is renowned in France but who has a bad reputation. He could indeed coin expressions like 'the heroes who put out the fire' to say 'firemen' or 'the riders pulling a chariot' simply to say people in a cart. In truth, I think that the metaphorical relation such as you portray it, taken by itself, is wholly unable to distinguish a bad comparison – perhaps denoting firemen with 'these valiant mortals who put out the fire' – from a good one. In one case, we have a metaphor, that is to say, a process that results in another manner of speaking. That is what we also do, in certain tongues, when we want a novel to talk about sexual themes. We take other words and make comparisons because there is a prohibition, because there is a moral barrier, but these other words are much poorer ones. So it seems to me that the true criterion for knowing whether a set of words works aesthetically is its relation to the totality of the projected object. Personally, I addressed the aesthetic problem only because Piovene and I were talking about subjectivity in art, but by that I did not mean to suggest that subjectivity defines the

17 Jacques Delille (1738–1813), translator of Virgil's *Georgics*. His most famous poem is *Les jardins, ou, L'art d'embellir les paysages* (1782), a poem in four 'songs'. He was as rapidly forgotten as he was famous in his own lifetime.

structure of art. But if we get to the true problem, then you cannot make an artistic critique independently of the totality, and you cannot consider the slightest phrase or formula apart from as a differentiation within this totality itself; which, moreover, is a totality linked to this other totality, language.

We must start out from totality – that is, the projected totality – and not only from this totality, but from the totality of a language [*langue*]. '*La notte si consumò*' [that is, Della Volpe's translation of 'So wore night'] is a phrase that works in Italian. We cannot say '*La nuit se consume*' in French. The poet who said '*La nuit se consume*' would not be a poet: his choice of words would be no good. Simply because there is a difference between these languages. And here I want to get to this point: this verse is by Browning, and though you can put it like this in English and translate it like that in Italian, we would certainly not translate Browning's poem into French by saying '*La nuit se consume*'. Simply because – and this is my point – languages [*langues*] implicate subjectivity. That is what we began to understand, ever since Saussure. What do we understand by subjectivity, in relation to languages? We understand this: that every fact, every fact of exteriority is interiorised in a total system and takes on an internal meaning, that is, one relating the whole to the part, whereas outside of this it was something else. And language [*langage*] in the form of languages [*langues*] is this: it is an ensemble structured by itself, with the phonological element, the lexical element, the semantic element, each of which conditions each other, and always synthetically and dialectically; and everything that happens in a language happens to it linguistically. That is, a language reflects all social facts, but it reflects them in its own manner as a language, and there will be new linguistic differentiations internal to the totality. Let's take the example of two invasions. When the Romans invaded and occupied Gaul it was the Latin language that prevailed. When the Normans invaded England, it was the English language that prevailed, with a few exceptions. In each of the two cases, the invasions were reflected in the language, not through ready-made facts but through new syntheses, new dialectical forms that introduced themselves, a new relation among words; but these were very particular relations that made this language into something without equivalents – and that makes it difficult to translate poems. So when you talk about a poet, you are entirely correct: it is a man who expresses the incommunicable by way of a subjective whole, the language [*langue*] – because he apprehends it, because the language is also an objectivating fact. For example, we cannot translate the difference between 'mutton' and 'sheep' into French [both are *mouton*]; and similarly we would cause you a lot of trouble with our word *bois*, which simultaneously means wood for the fire, a forest, etc. [it has no Italian equivalent].

So we have the poet who uses these elements, but these elements are not uniquely objective structures – they are simultaneously both objective and subjective, and subjective in an intersubjective sense. So in the artistic fact we have the structured totality that the poet wants to create by way of another structured intersubjective totality, namely the language [*langue*]. We can never translate Mayakovsky: there are some translations by Elsa Triolet, which can get as close as you like, but you don't feel the . . .

A VOICE: The impossibility of translating – well, there's a romantic argument!

SARTRE: No, it is a provisional thesis; but it is a fact that at the current moment we don't translate poems, the great poets; we don't translate them. We translate certain parts where there is a kind of approximation, but other parts we don't: and some of them are truly, totally, untranslatable. I'll give you one example, and it's a very curious one, because he's a great poet. Now, if you take his words the one after the other, if you take what he says, it's truly lamentable: I'm talking about Lamartine. In truth Lamartine is not very interesting to read, but it is poetry. It's a certain type of poetry of his era.

A VOICE: Rather a mediocre poet!

SARTRE: No, a good poet, but one who said mediocre things. That happens to a lot of poets. And you cannot translate Lamartine into another language.

A VOICE: The same goes for Pushkin.

SARTRE: That's another poet who it's impossible to translate. And Mayakovsky, too, it's impossible to translate him into French. And your poets? Petrarch, impossible, it would be senseless. And Shakespeare? In truth, I agree with you that all this is temporary, since it represents a moment: history is not universal, it begins to be universal, it is not completely universal. But this is not a romantic myth, it is a reality, and a reality that I have constantly come up against. I simply wanted to suggest to you that if we want to talk about works of art, then we first have to speak of the idea of totality and the idea of projection towards a totality by way of totalitarian fields, one of which – and on that you're entirely right – is language [*le langage*]. But properly taking into account the fact that the choice of words comes from the totality, and it is then subject to this other totality that is language. In particular, the surrealists in France often made for very good poets, very great poets, but they were also poets without metaphor. In their case, you can't take recourse to the 'the night passes' behind 'so wore night'. That's not what they wanted. They wanted something quite different. The surrealists wanted to set some words directly next to others that had no logical connection to them, in order to get hold of something that is, or in any case should give you, an objective reality that is simultaneously rationally comprehensible. Isn't that right? Take the example, if you will, of the 'butter horse'. They wrote of a 'butter horse': a horse, then, that would melt in the sun, a horse that could be eaten. Their goal was clearly a sort of self-destruction of language [*langage*] by itself, allowing us to look for what's behind it: I am not telling you that they were right or wrong. Poetically, this example is not well-chosen; but they often were right, poetically. Fine, but where does this butter horse take us? Only to horses and to butter: that is, not to expressions, but to the signifying differentiations in language.

A VOICE: Let's take Pushkin, where he says 'Unscathed by northern gales blooms the Russian rose'.[18] Here there is no metaphor, but the same thing is at work here, the dialectical relation between . . .

SARTRE: Ah, yes, here there is no metaphor, there is a real. It's just that at this moment it is the whole that counts, totality; the totality decides whether you use a metaphorical ensemble . . .

---

18 The speaker says '*comme s'ouvre legère la rose russe dans le tourbillon de la neige*', a reference that the French editors ascribe to Pushkin's *Winter Morning*. However, it seems more likely that this in fact is a rendering of line 45 from his *Winter: What Are We to Do in the Country?* (Зима. Что делать нам в деревне?), which reads 'Но бури севера не вредны русской розе' – DB.

A VOICE: But won't I find that the same is true for a passage of Mommsen's?

SARTRE: Yes! But the difference between Mommsen and the poet is that there is an objective ensemble that allows other historians to come along and pull apart Mommsen's evaluation of certain points. So then Mommsen will be reduced to [*renvoyé à*] his subjectivity, like – as I was telling you yesterday – our friend who suggested *Le Grabuge* [as a journal title], and who was reduced to his subjectivity because this proposal was not accepted. Whereas no one would ever think of reproaching Pushkin for having been a poet, saying that he had been transcended, or reproaching Flaubert for having written *Madame Bovary*. There is a difference, in the sense that the work of art is an absolute: if it is a good one, it remains so; it cannot be transcended, it would be meaningless to say that. Mommsen's work can be transcended because it is on the level of rigorously objective truth, whereas the work of art is an absolute, precisely because you will never transcend the incarnation of a singular individual. Flaubert was not a very pleasant figure, not someone who you wish you'd been; he died almost a hundred years ago, etc., in a period that was less advanced than our own in all sorts of ways. That said, *Madame Bovary* remains something that is entirely impossible to transcend, because Flaubert is in it. Whereas, if he had described the society without putting himself into it, it would be a description that we could pick up retrospectively and develop further, as Luporini said; and clearly it would then have a wholly different meaning, however valuable it was as an ensemble. I am simply warning you against separating out the structures of subjectivity too much: all this makes up a whole.

I would add that it's not accurate to say that I am mounting a phenomenological description. That's not the task that I have set myself. Rather, what is at issue is to find – by way of a regressive dialectic – the fields of internal meanings that allow us to understand the work of art projectively. When, for example, Flaubert started to consider himself a woman, we have to know how come, when he was almost fifty-five years old and a doctor said to him, 'You are a hysterical old woman', rather than getting angry, he was delighted, and how come in all his letters he wrote 'you'll never guess what they told me – they tell me that I am a hysterical old woman'. We have to understand this; and it's not that he was a homosexual.

So here is a certain kind of guy who we can't understand by description, but by . . .

A VOICE: . . . psychoanalysis.

SARTRE: Ah, of course, psychoanalysis. Indeed I don't see why it should be rejected, as long as it doesn't have a metaphysical basis, as long as it doesn't say (as it sometimes does) that it can explain capitalism in terms of some complex, for example. But if we take psychoanalysis simply as a method for objectivating subjectivity, then I don't at all see why it should be rejected. And what does psychoanalysis teach us, when we take it dialectically? It teaches us about the personal adventure of an individual within a family, through his first years. But what does this adventure represent? It singularly represents the society of a given era. For example, the Oedipus complex – that is, the child's relation with his mother and antagonistic relation with his father – has no sense for the eighteenth century.

For example, if you read Rétif de la Bretonne's *Mémoires*, then you will see that he was fixated – as a psychoanalyst would say – on his father, whereas his mother was not of great importance. And take Flaubert: for him it was his father who counted, because again his was a family of this same era. Conversely, Baudelaire, who was born in a richer, more cultured and more bourgeois family, was fixated on his mother, because already there was this shift in the family . . . And what does that mean? It means that the domestic family, broken by the rise of capitalism, was transforming into the normal bourgeois family, the conjugal family. That's something very important, and so your psychoanalysis of a singular life is only reflecting a situation that is objective and social.

A VOICE: We still haven't got to the work of art . . .

SARTRE: But this is very important, because it's starting from here that you get to a singular work of art.

LUPORINI: I just wanted to observe that I have read Della Volpe's books. His position and Sartre's are not really so far apart – within limits, of course. Della Volpe defines the work of art as a closed discourse, and scientific discourse as an open discourse. I think that if we had started the discussion from this point – that is, on the plane of totality, of the interpretation of totality – that would have been more productive. I wanted to ask for Sartre's response to a question that concerns the great problem of the permanence of art's value. That is the question Marx posed. I do not accept the answer that Marx gave, but I do agree that it's the right question. I think that to define the work of art as an absolute, in the sense that Sartre has just suggested, does not suffice to answer this problem. The work of art can be an absolute, but this is an absolute that does not interest us, an absolute that concerns the subject that created it. But what is at issue is the permanence of the value of a work of art, the thing that makes the poems of the *Iliad* and the *Odyssey* maintain all their value even for us – we have to constantly reconquer it, for sure, but it is always there. I think that this problem is linked to the difference in the form, the difference in type, between artistic knowledge and scientific knowledge, etc.

SARTRE: Well, I would say that it's precisely because art is a closed discourse, in the sense that you have projected from the singularised society onto a totality, which is the description of this same society. We never demand, so to speak, that a work of art give us objective information on a period. Rather, we ask that it give us a more complex type of information: again, not objective information, but its duplication of a period seeing itself, with all its possible blindnesses, all its prejudices – yet, at the same time, experiencing itself, no? What it represents is a totalisation of the period in the form of the individual or group of individuals who made it. Take for example *Don Quixote*: what is it that makes *Don Quixote* an enduring work? There is a historical aspect that may interest only historians: the liquidation of a certain feudal society. In an era when absolute monarchies were establishing themselves – and, as such, at the same time as the Renaissance – here we also have the liquidation of a feudal ideology in favour of another ideology, within a man who lived this contradiction. The liquidation of this feudalism – in the form of tales of chivalry, regarding a man who would now simply be a soldier for the king and no longer a wandering knight – is interesting from a strictly historical point of view, if that's how we take it. But if we read this in a book into which a man has projected these contradictions, then we have to deal with a character like Don Quixote – who is almost constantly ridiculous and sometimes tragic – isn't that right? With this kind of strange contradiction that is Cervantes's own. There we have something that interests us, because it presents us with this whole society as a society that is as lively in its contradictions as the one that we live in.

Do you see what I am getting at? *Don Quixote* would not be able to connect to us if it were not for Cervantes's subjectivity, and precisely in the way that Cervantes was very ill at ease in himself, because he was witnessing this separation between two worlds. So, for my part – and I would like to say this, too – I don't think that a historical character is a historical type. I don't think that the true goal of a novel – or, at least, of a typical character in a novel – is 'typologising'. Rather, I think that its goal is the singularisation of the universal. But singularisation of the universal does not mean typical. It means presenting us a character who in himself – like Don Quixote, for example – is in no sense typical. But in reality, I think it is necessary to represent characters who have a certain degree of obscurity at the outset, which is their individuality, their personality, and whose universality the reader gradually succeeds in discovering concretely, though without ever arriving at the universal in itself. If you see what I mean by that.

Moreover, it is necessary that the character – like Don Quixote, for example – be plagued by manias, a sort of imbecility that strikes right from the outset: that he behave unusually, like a one-in-a-thousand case. And then, without him ceasing to be unusual, we should be able to feel all the contradictions of his era within him. So you have this constant fact, the real and individual fact of the life of each person, namely, that we are incarnations; that is to say, that we are the singularisation of the whole universal of systems within which we live. We are that – each of us is – and that is what our novels show. If we are presented as living in full awareness of what the contradictions are, that does not ring true. However, if we are presented as beings who do not recognise these contradictions, which are half-hidden – we can grasp them in part, but in part we can't – then we are on the terrain of the work of art. Whatever the degree of abstraction or schematisation, here we find the character that each of us is, for ourselves and for others.

A VOICE [LUPORINI?]: Excuse me, Sartre, but I don't think that suffices to answer the question of the permanence of the value of a work of art, which is linked to the work's existence, its presence. For example, in an archaeological dig I found a fragment of a work of art from a civilisation that I don't know anything about – but that, to my eyes, is a work of art, and so the fragment immediately took on an artistic value. All that poses problems of interpretation. It is the immediate incarnation of a value and the permanence of a value, which is something completely different from historical values, etc. And that's the problem that Marx posed, and I still haven't found any answer to it, either in you or in Della Volpe or in Lukács, or in general.

SARTRE: Yes, but then I'd say this. On the one hand, you can't provide an answer to that without an analysis and a study of the work itself. It is impossible to say, in principle, why one work endures and another does not. That's a problem that concerns the work itself. On the other hand, what is missing, in my view . . .

A VOICE: That is a general problem . . .

SARTRE: Yes, that is a general problem, but it's one that can only be resolved by particular studies. You cannot decide *a priori*. And second, both you and we are still lacking a theory of values. Marxism does not have a theory of values. You are missing any such theory. So to you Marxists I say that there is no established Marxist axiological system; indeed, there is no such system – we cannot claim to have found one, either. To be clear, that is still not a given. It's not true, it is still not a given. Evidently a Marxist axiology does need to be created: it is one of the essential questions. There are elements of it, but it is not a given. So you pose a problem that I think is almost premature, because you want to found this permanence on values, but we have to find these values, establish what they are.

A VOICE: Even Marx . . .

SARTRE: But he didn't have the values for a response; we still need to know how in a Marxist system – like that which we discussed today and yesterday, or how thousands of others have defined it before us – how, in this system, the passage to value, in short, to a norm, can exist. That isn't already given. And also there is almost always a contradiction – a well-founded contradiction, but still a constant one – between a Marxist's judgement on an individual and his activity, for example, and the dialectical understanding of this individual as the actual representative of a fraction, of a class, acting as he must act on this basis. There is a problem, here, and this problem has never been dealt with. Yes, from 1945 to 1952 there were abusive versions of value judgements, but there wasn't the foundation for value judgements. And then there is the reaction – precisely because we made too many unfounded value judgements in this period – that consists of creating a Marxism without values, in which people are what they are, produced by economic and historical processes. That doesn't work either, and it suffocates any possibility of judging either action or the work of art.

So I believe that this is one of the problems we have; indeed, it is linked to subjectivity, but not . . .

A VOICE: In my philosophical training, I started out with the masterpiece. So I am going to explain my thinking to see if I am truly in agreement. The task is to explicate a Marxist axiological theory . . .

SARTRE: Exactly.

A VOICE: . . . in which the subject, the question of art must have its place . . .

SARTRE: And also a moral . . .

A VOICE: Of course.

SARTRE: But this is an extremely difficult problem, since we could also say that the moral is not possible in the current state of things, that is, with men whose relations are reified, with fetishes, with a struggle that is in itself a violent struggle. We could say that today the moral is impossible, and at the same time that it has to be, if we want to give account of all aspects of humanity.

In my view the two problems are analogous. For example, if I told you that it is clear that in certain circumstances no moral attitude can be taken. Let's imagine a young man who has become a colonial administrator because he just drifted into this position, or because his family forced him to, and here he is in the colonies. He cannot apply any kind of moral attitude, among the colonised who he is administering. Even if he was as liberal as liberal could be, this would be a liberal neocolonialism. He couldn't do anything. Similarly, in the relation between a married couple, if one of the two is totally alienated then the other can't do anything. I have even seen cases where the wife was alienated and the husband wanted her to work, and this – quite proper – attitude in fact led the wife to become even more alienated, because she was working out of obedience to her husband. So either all problems are totally turned inside-out by the current situation, by the current separation, by the current world, or else there is no real possibility of moral action or of axiology. And nonetheless it is impossible to speak for anyone for fifteen minutes without letting out thirty-odd axiological judgements. So we have to take account of that. And there has never been any serious prospect of a rigorous Marxist work on that.

Reality and Objectivity

SARTRE: Given that we're about to go our separate ways, I think that the most useful thing to do now would be to pin down what points we have reached agreements on, and which other ones represented points of disagreement. And also, to note the problems that none of us could claim to provide any resolution to, but which were simply problems that we posed. I cannot myself say what the agreements and disagreements are – I would rather that all of us discussed them together. For example, right away I'll address myself to Luporini, because I think that this is the starting point. I think that you above all addressed the problem of subjectivity in knowledge, and I elaborated more on subjectivity in *praxis*, or in the practical or affective relation with the people who surround us, but we would agree in saying that subjectivity is an indispensable moment in the passage to objectivation. Would you accept that much, in this form? I think that this is an essential point. I don't think that we agree on what comes next, namely the way in which we ought to envisage this passage and this moment. But it seems to me that we have seen this – the real dialectical process passing from a material being to an objective being – because we cannot call a material being an objective being, seeing that the objective is always linked to the subjective. The passage from the material being – in its real but still not objective form – to its objective, social form, with all the contradictions that this will then imply, supposes the subjective moment, in the group as in the individual. I would like to know if you would accept this initial conclusion, in these terms, or perhaps with modifications.

LUPORINI: Thank you very much for posing the questions in this manner, that is, in giving us the opportunity to respond. To be frank, I have to say that I accept this answer only in part. I do accept the fact that there is a moment of objectivation, which evidently depends on subjectivity, and I accept the fact that subjectivity is absolutely ineliminable, always ineliminable. As concerns the other point, that is, the question of whether we can speak of objectivity only within this relation – in a relation of objectivation – I can't agree. I know that there is a very difficult problem, here . . .

SARTRE: A problem of words and of . . .

LUPORINI: It's not a question of words.

SARTRE: I mean, words in the sense that words are paired with concepts. I'll quote you this phrase from Vigier,[1] 'If man disappeared, the internal relations between the nucleus of the atom

1 Jean-Pierre Vigier (1920–2004), a French physicist and political activist, and a member of the PCF from 1940 to 1969. Active in the anti-Nazi Resistance, he was a prominent opponent of the US intervention in Vietnam and general secretary of the Russell Tribunal, as well as actively participating in May '68. As a physicist he worked at the CEA [Atomic Energy Commission] from its foundation together with Frédéric Joliot-Curie, before leaving for the CNRS [National Scientific Research Council], where he was Louis de Broglie's assistant. He defended a materialist and determinist position. We could not find a reference for this quote, but other references allow us to confirm that it does respect the spirit of Vigier's arguments.

and its elements would preserve their objective reality'. For me, such a sentence is meaningless. They would, naturally, preserve their real relations, but for whom would they be objects? They have to be objects for someone, or, in any case, for some organism, perhaps a different one to our own.

LUPORINI: I think that's an excellent way of posing the question. In posing the question of an objectivity without man, we pose a theological question.

SARTRE: Absolutely. There's nothing left but God!

LUPORINI: But if we shift from this position to the opposite one, there is still the danger of passing into idealist territory.

SARTRE: But that's what we have to avoid.

LUPORINI: That's what I see in you a little, I'll say that very frankly. I think that here we have a problem of the *medium*, a *medium* situation. You yourself have used the word 'real'; so let's see what the 'real' is. We cannot think about what the 'real' is without referring to something that is in the background of objectivity. And I can't say that I already have the answer to this problem . . .

SARTRE: No, but in any case I would say that reality is already something that is not idealist. The solar system's existence doesn't require man;[2] it is a fact that in relation to the solar

2 Sartre's argument would be more consistent if he said 'For the solar system to *be*, it doesn't require man'. Up to this point, he practised a distinction whereby the real belongs to the order of being, and the objective to the order of existence.

system, we are contingent. If you like, it is perhaps necessary that the development of life on planet Earth leads to us; but in relation to the entire system, our existence or disappearance does not count, at least from the viewpoint of astronomical studies. If you accept that, as you surely will, then there is no idealism. We have to conceive the world as not made for man – it is not made in expectation of man.[3]

LUPORINI: Agreed.

SARTRE: After all, that's the reality.

LUPORINI: So in this situation, which you accept, there is a world before man and without man.

SARTRE: Evidently.

LUPORINI: And the objectivation that starts from consciousness, and which I proceed towards as a practical movement? There's a relation that is not only a relation at the level of thought, at the level of theoretical reflection, but a relation that has established itself. I only know this *a posteriori*, but it has established itself in the very development of reality.

SARTRE: I agree entirely.

LUPORINI: There are intermediate levels, which have established themselves as intermediate levels . . .

---

3 See Jean-Paul Sartre, 'Vérité et existence', in *Essais*, Paris: Gallimard, 1948, p. 83: '. . . the word is human but not anthropomorphic'.

SARTRE: But all the same, at a given moment they have to be taken back by interiority . . .

LUPORINI: . . . but which mean that my movement towards objectivation is always, at the same time, the conquest of a real objectivity, an objectivity that really exists . . .

SARTRE: Of a reality that exists, a reality that is part of objectivity, but not of an objectivity . . .

LUPORINI: We could simply say: there is an objectivity constituted for man; I believe that it is constituted for man already according to the order of magnitude of his existence. That is, it is more or less the same objectivity constituted for the biological being. This objectivity is not only constituted on the basis of the immediate reflection of the world in man's interiority, but it is simultaneously constituted on the basis of this objectivity, which you call the real, which is man: we can call this objectivity no. one, as to avoid using the same word and causing confusion . . .

SARTRE: But why use the word 'objectivity' at this point at all? When the word 'reality' is more full . . .

LUPORINI: Because then there wouldn't be this movement through which I objectivate a thing and from which I emerge as a biological being.

SARTRE: On that we completely agree. Yes – it's just that this emergence takes place in the form of a retotalisation.

LUPORINI: I want to say something very serious, if I may. There is an *in-itself* [*un en soi*] of objectivity, an *itself* [*un soi*], an *In-sich*, of objectivity, an *in-itself* of the part of the object that I do not just *acquire* but *conquer* through this movement.

SARTRE: Merleau-Ponty would grant you that.

LUPORINI: You can't forget that. Without that, you can't explain, for example, that science is always an approximation. When we say that science is an approximation, we are posing a very serious question, and we cannot say that this is a scientific position. So there are realities that are still to be defined: a human reality, the movement of the unconscious . . .

SARTRE: Yes, but then, indeed, you are very much defining objectivity in relation to subjectivity in the sense that I understand it. You are saying, in sum, that there is something behind and something ahead, and, in each case you call that *in-itself* [*en soi*]. But precisely the point is that the *in-itself* isn't for us: there is the *in-itself*, and then there is the *for others* [*pour autrui*], the *for us* [*pour nous*], or the *for itself* [*pour soi*].

LUPORINI: There is the passage, which is called . . .

SARTRE: Well, the passage, or the *for us*, is made by subjectivity; and when, at a given moment, you mark the limits of a science, in my view you are marking, if you will, the intersubjective limits of human knowledge.[4] Why do we stop

4 For Antonio Gramsci, objectivity means intersubjectivity: 'The point that must be made against [Nikolai Bukharin's 1921] *Popular Manual* is that it has presented the subjectivist conception just as it appears from the point of view of common-sense criticism and that it has adopted the conception of the objective reality of the external world in its most trivial and uncritical sense without so much as a suspicion that it can run into objections on the grounds of mysticism, as indeed it has. However, if

there, after all? Because we have such-and-such history that we have retotalised in a certain way with such-and-such instruments and principles. Hence our subjectivity relating to a reality that in every sense goes beyond it, but which will be conquered, I agree, little by little, through historical stages, which must always be considered subjective. To put it another way, there is a subjectivity of science, which is the fact that it is there and in this moment, and not somewhere else. This is not at all an idealist subjectivity, since it comes from the entire development of the organic being, the social being, the instruments created on the basis of our *praxis*, and the theory that enlightens it. But ultimately we are like that at each moment, and our successors,

---

one analyses this idea it is not all that easy to justify a view of external objectivity understood in such a mechanical way. It might seem that there can exist an extra-historical and extrahuman objectivity. But who is the judge of such objectivity? . . . It can indeed be maintained that here we are dealing with a hangover of the concept of God, precisely in its mystic form of a conception of an unknown God. . . . Objective always means "humanly objective" which can be held to correspond exactly to "historically subjective": in other words, objective would mean "universal subjective". Man knows objectively in so far as knowledge is real for the whole human race historically unified in a single unitary cultural system. But this process of historical unification takes place through the disappearance of the internal contradictions which tear apart human society'. Antonio Gramsci, *Selections from the Prison Notebooks*, London: Lawrence and Wishart, 1971, pp. 444–5.

The Italian Communist leader and thinker Antonio Gramsci (1891–1937) participated in the founding of the Communist Party of Italy (PCI) and became its general secretary in 1924. He was imprisoned under the Mussolini regime from 1926 until 1937, and died a few days after his release. During his eleven years of captivity he composed his *Prison Notebooks*. We could hardly hope to present Gramsci's thought in a footnote, and thus we will limit ourselves to highlighting that he elaborated a philosophy of *praxis*, as against an objectivist or naturalist interpretation of materialism such as we find in Engels. This reference to the expression 'philosophy of praxis' itself shows the theoretical and political interest that there would be in propounding a systematic comparative analysis of Gramsci's and Sartre's reasoning.

the people who will come after us will say 'you know, our grandparents still believed that!' And they will blame that on our subjectivity, indeed as we do in relation to the people of the Middle Ages. All the same, I believe that on this point we could . . .

LUPORINI: We could discuss that for hours, but there is still a difference, namely the objectivity of subjectivity – the original objectivity of subjectivity, to be precise. Evidently, there are things that I cannot see, except through reflection.

SARTRE: But by that do you mean that in its origin [*originellement*] subjectivity has some relation to the object? I am totally in agreement on that, you can't conceive of it otherwise . . .

LUPORINI: That's the idealist response.

SARTRE: Or do you mean that subjectivity is more than a moment of a reality through which the being-in-itself is then constituted as objective? To put that another way, do you mean that there is an objective *in-itself*?

LUPORINI: I want to say that a real, objective relation between a being that subjectivises me and an inert being . . .

A VOICE: The discussion keeps identifying objectivity and reality, so what about the linguistic distinction that you're calling for? Objectivity is not reality.

SARTRE: Do you associate – do you identify – objectivity and reality?

LUPORINI: No, I'm posing the question as to whether it is possible to speak of a reality without in some sense referring to subjectivity. That's the question.

SARTRE: It's impossible.

LUPORINI: So long as we haven't defined reality, what we can say is that reality is one thing and objectivity is another . . .

SARTRE: It is impossible, practically, in the sense that everything that we know in a rigorous manner is determinate, is objective. But when you speak of something that is always beyond, beyond approximation, it is a reality that is still not objective, because it exists for us only as the objective and subjective limit to our experience. When we were talking about Michelson and Morley the other day, we said that we can interpret certain principles as we like, but at a certain point Michelson and Morley's experiment must enter into consideration. And what is it that their experiment gives us? It gives us light moving at constant speed in all directions. It's in complete contradiction with Newton's system. That makes for a contradiction. Not a contradiction in reality, but a human contradiction, in knowledge. What does that show us? Either that science doesn't exist, which is absurd, or else that there is something that we haven't understood. Do you really think that we can call this reality – which escapes us, and manifests itself only through the contradiction in our knowledge – an objectivity? I call it a reality. In the same sense, today a subquantum mechanics is emerging in which we see that particles transform into each other in regions of high energy. But all the scholars occupied with this question agree: we don't currently have any mathematical materials to deal with this question. That is, we use phrases and formulas somewhat haphazardly, leaving things a little to chance or to a bit of cleverness, in order to grasp the reality; we don't completely succeed in doing so. This reality does totally exist as a reality, outside of us, and yet for us it has only a relative objectivity – this objectivity is not developed, it is not total. We know that these particles exist, but we don't have the means really to know them. We will do so in ten or twenty years, and to know that they exist does mark progress in objectivity, but they are enormously troubling for science as a whole; it is one of the reasons why science is in crisis, because it doesn't have the means to deal with this. When Vigier talks about it, for example, he discusses it in the form of a condition to be fulfilled. I would call that an objectivity in progress, in movement, an implicit objectivity that will be explicated, but not a true objectivity. That said, it is an absolute reality, it does exist, and if we did not exist it would still exist. It is in this sense that you can't call this idealism, because idealism consists of saying that its being owes to it being perceived, in one way or another.

AFTERWORD: SARTRE'S ACTUALITY

By Fredric Jameson

Sartré's Actuality

Reading the transcript of Sartre's Rome lecture – along with the discussion that followed it – confronts us with an alternative which, while undecidable, opens up multiple interpretations. For it is on the one hand the record of an event, the encounter between the Sartre of the *Critique of Dialectical Reason*, already involved in his work on Flaubert, and a number of important Italian Marxists, many of them members of the Italian Communist Party, at the Gramsci Institute in Rome in 1961. This is then an interaction of great historical interest: documenting Sartre's approach to the Communist Party fully as much as his approach to Marxism itself – the Italian Party being a good deal more hospitable to such an exchange of views than the French one – and also testifying to the vitality and the variety of philosophical commitments of the Italian Marxism of this period.

But the text is also a philosophical statement, or series of statements, betraying the continuity between *Being and Nothingness* and the *Critique*, and the Hegelian affinities of the latter, but also shedding interesting light on Sartre's position on subjectivity and his evident insistence on the non-subjectivist—and non-idealist—nature of his thinking. Meanwhile, the debate that followed also elicited significant interventions by major Italian thinkers, from Enzo Paci and Cesare Luporini to Galvano Della Volpe and Lucio Colletti. Unsurprisingly, the exchanges often turn on very familiar themes in the history of Marxist polemics: most notably the distinction between historical and dialectical materialisms – or in other words, between a Kantian or Viconian position on what human knowledge can achieve and a materialist philosophy which affirms the dialectic of nature itself. Sartre will be both reserved and conciliatory on this matter, often seen as the fundamental sticking-point in any opposition between Western or non-Communist Marxism and the more 'orthodox' kind. He allows that some laws of nature may be discovered that are dialectical, but draws back from any affirmation of a single dialectic of Nature as such; and also politely asks whether the hotly contested word 'reflexion' – *Widerspiegelung*, or the 'reflexion theory of knowledge' – might not tactically be replaced by something less controversial like 'adequation'.

There is then an inclusive engagement over the idea of contradiction (this will be a particularly significant issue in Colletti's thought); a rather emphatic insistence on Sartre's part on the lack of any ethical dimension or theory of value in Marxist philosophy; and a rather wilful diversion of the discussion into the area of art and aesthetics, in which Sartre offers the case of *Madame Bovary* as a fundamental exhibit of the way in which the significant work of art has dimensions which are simultaneously subjective and objective; while Della Volpe draws extended attention to the problems of poetic language as such. The 'debate' then amicably concludes with agreement on the need for a 'critical Communism' – an expression Balibar will revive some thirty years later, with a small *c* and a quite different meaning.

Fifty years on

It is a coincidence which reminds us that, whichever perspective we adopt in our approach to this text – as a historical event or a philosophical statement – we cannot but add a third one, namely our positions as readers some fifty years after the fact, in a situation in which both politics and philosophy have undergone radical transformations, and in which our reception of this debate must itself face an alternative: namely whether to read it relatively neutrally, for its interest as an event in the intellectual history of the past, or to interrogate it for its relevance in the current environment, where Marxist theory has returned to an emphasis on the more purely economic issues of crisis theory and the structure of a globalised late capitalism, while philosophy has either passed into a more post-individualist, linguistic or metaphysical problematic – with the work of a Deleuze or a Badiou, or even the Lacanians – or has returned to Kantian questions with a vengeance.

For all of these contemporary tendencies, Sartre has several red flags to wave. The very emphasis of the debate on subjectivity – at least according to its initial intentions and programme – will reawaken all the post-existential and Althusserian hostility to the various phenomenological conceptions of experience. The vocabulary of 'totalisation' developed in the *Critique of Dialectical Reason* will arouse now perhaps ancient or dormant repudiations of notions of totality as such, despite the fact that Sartre's term was meant to substitute a process and an activity for this inert and substantified noun; and without any particularly scandalised awareness of its continuing use, in only slightly modified form, in the Deleuzian trinity of territorialisation, deterritorialisation and reterritorialisation. Finally, Sartre's belated deployment of the term 'freedom' may well awaken more purely philosophical critiques of this notion, less as an exceedingly stringent account of the dilemmas of the for-itself, than as a well-nigh Kantian barrier to that collective ethics he here demands, but which never really overcame the abstraction of the categorical imperative, something of which his occasional use of the word 'humanism' also reminds us, in this post-Khrushchevian and post-Stalinist Marxist theoretical discussion.

The Italian interlocutors do not seize upon what seems to me the fundamental weakness of this moment of Sartre's thought: what I venture to call its 'monadic' tendency, what Althusser denounced, in Hegel and others – who no doubt also included Lukács and even the tutelary deity of this gathering, namely Gramsci himself – as the fallacy of an 'expressive' totality, the notion that within a given particular the whole of a social or historical moment is somehow included, and might be available to hermeneutic exploration and display, as Sartre tried to do in his biographical works, or 'existential psychoanalyses'. This view presupposes what he calls incarnation: 'which means that each individual is, in a certain fashion, the total representation of his/her epoch' – a social being 'lives the whole social order from his/her point of view'. It is true that he adds the words 'an individual, whoever it is, or a group, or some sort of assembly, is an incarnation of the total society', which might lead us on to those discussions of class and class consciousness only fleetingly touched on in the opening debate. This biographical perspective of Sartre's final project has been described as something like the ultimate revenge of his starting point, in the individual cogito and in a description of phenomenological experience; yet paradoxically, Heidegger's *Being and Time*, resolutely avoiding Cartesian or humanist language, seems to end up in the same blind alley, which determines his famous *Kehre*.

I have raised this issue not to launch a philosophical critique of Sartre, but rather to point out how different our philosophical discussions and preoccupations are today, where, in the multiple institutionalised environments of late capitalism and globalisation, the existential choices of this or that individual and the biographical adventures of this or that freedom seem to have become of very limited interest indeed. Even in the field of some properly Marxist research, the concept of ideology has fallen into disrepute, and the relationship of the individual to class and to class consciousness takes second place to the problem of classes themselves: whether they still exist and how they might be called upon to act if they do. Yet it was precisely to the analysis of group and class dynamics that the *Critique of Dialectical Reason* summoned us and devoted its most productive energies.

As to whether we can expect a Sartre 'revival' to challenge the ongoing and often vacuous invocation of Heidegger one still finds everywhere in contemporary thought, I can testify that younger readers are still electrified by the descriptions of *Being and Nothingness* and readily acknowledge the phenomenological and philosophical truth of its accounts of freedom; yet its terminology no longer seems to generate the fresh problems the institution of philosophy demands of its solutions. Instead, it seems to be the first Sartre, of the *Transcendence of the Ego*, which has again achieved philosophical actuality, in its insistence on the impersonality of consciousness and its displacement of the 'self' and of personal identity: this short essay indeed may be said to have heralded that structuralist and post-structuralist 'death of the subject' which is still very much with us today.

Meanwhile, the later Sartre of the *Critique of Dialectical Reason* compellingly raises the inverse problem, namely that of the 'identity' of groups and collectives in a biological situation where 'collective consciousness' is clearly an unacceptable concept. Those pages of the *Critique*, therefore, in which Sartre contrasts the small-group dynamics of guerrilla or nomadic units with the serial alienation of larger public-opinion-type collectives, still have an unparalleled urgency, both political and philosophical, today. How these two features of Sartre's thought then are related is one of the important lessons the Rome lecture holds for us.

Language and praxis

Terminology is still the surest thread to guide us through the labyrinth of philosophical development, provided we interrogate it both ways: what dilemmas does the new terminology allow us to exclude or to neutralise, and what unique insights does the new formulation blur or occlude? Both Sartre and Heidegger meant firmly to avoid the illusions of subjectification: Heidegger did it by strenuously banning the language of consciousness and of personification; Sartre, the other way round, by insisting so strongly on the language of consciousness that the personalised languages of identity and the self could find no place in his formulations. Sartre's new language of totalisation is then a kind of assimilation of the so-called 'pragmatic Heidegger': it develops the notion of consciousness as a project both by enlarging it, to include the Heideggerian conception of world, and worldness and 'worlding', and by describing the ways in which my ongoing temporality draws everything around itself into a *Zuhandenheit* – a tool-like 'readiness to hand' – quite different from the older static and contemplative epistemological philosophies of objects and their purely knowable presence (*Vorhandenheit*).

But for contemporary thought, for which difference is more congenial than identity, the term 'totalisation' seemed to place a premium on unification; whereas we want our subjects to be multiple and heterogeneous, and prefer incommensurable subject-positions to any of those perspectives of unification – even in perpetual process – from which some ultimately reunified subject or self might arise. Today's readers will therefore be relieved to know that Sartre here insists – and it is perhaps the most striking moment of the whole discussion – that subjectivity is an evanescent phenomenon: a moment and not a structure or an essence, and indeed a moment that almost at once loses itself in objectivity again, in the world and in action in it. But this insistence comes at a different and perhaps no less onerous price, namely that of Hegelianism.

For the language of the *Critique* in which Sartre couches his description of 'subjectivity' – all the while refusing this term and reminding us of Hegel's own warning about the deleterious effect of the existence of two separate words for subject and object – is nonetheless a profoundly Hegelian one, in which we exteriorise or externalise ourselves and then 'return' back into the self in order to prepare a new exteriorisation. This is the omnipresent Hegelian process of objectivisation, from which the young Marx famously sought to distinguish its negative form in 'alienation', the way in which we make ourselves other to ourselves. 'Praxis', a word reinvented by Count Cieszkowski only some ten years after Hegel's death, is no doubt the Sartrean version of this Hegelian (and Goethean) *Tätigkeit*, or perpetual activity, which in Marx will become an ethic of production in the human rather than the industrial-capitalist sense.

In any case, this dialectic of the inside and the outside, of the transformation of the world which then returns on the self, transforming it in its turn, is by now a familiar trope or figure. What is modern and un-Hegelian in Sartre's exposition of it here is his emphasis on language, and the way in which language objectifies interiority, transforming its inwardness into something external which then in turn transforms its starting point in wordless subjectivity. This dialectic is now baptised reification (Sartre had already coined the rather barbarous term *chosification* in *Being and Nothingness*); and his examples – drawn from personal or everyday life and already rather novelistic – show why abstract or universalising theories of action and ethics are congenial to this novelist-philosopher. They also insist on language itself as a form of reification, for good or ill: Count Mosca's famous anxiety about the word 'love' demonstrates one way in which naming can suddenly transform everything. But characterological reification – the worker who discovers he is an anti-Semite, Leiris's inveterate crystallisations of his own rebellious and anarchistic inclinations – these bring the Sartrean dialectic of language much closer to psychoanalysis than his philosophical repudiation of a concept of the Unconscious would seem to imply. Indeed, the substitution for an entity named the Unconscious – something which makes for philosophical trouble for Freud, and which Lacan is obliged ingeniously to rewrite – of the past, as a kind of non-knowledge, sedimented in the body and not reducible only to some linguistically definable concept such as memory, may well have been more productive for Sartre, particularly in developing the insights of his biographies.

This is the point at which class appears and in which one would have thought the most productive dialogue with the Italian Marxists might have been pursued – alas, it was not. For Sartre's emphasis here is not on class struggle itself, as the inevitable conflict between social groups, and eventually between those two fundamental social groups which are the masters and the producers. Rather, it is with the historical forms of class consciousness within a given group that Sartre is concerned here, and how the externalisation of subjectivity in the shape of a specific kind of technology returns on the practitioners of that technology to form their own specific type of consciousness, which then in its turn returns into the social world of class conflict to play a specific kind of role. The example is the moment in which the class consciousness of skilled workers is threatened by a technology that no longer requires their skills and transforms the 'proletariat' into a mass of unskilled labour with a very different attitude towards work, politics and class struggle as such.

This is surely, for Marxists, the most interesting and subtle lesson in the Sartrean analysis of subjectivity today, where wholly new kinds of technology and labour have transformed our social life and seem to have left the older categories of social and political analysis behind them. For today, it is not particularly the notion of class struggle that needs reviving: we see it inescapably everywhere around us. What we need is some renewed awareness of what class consciousness itself is and how it functions. The Sartre of these early 1960s lectures has significant things to tell us about that.

Printed in the United States
by Baker & Taylor Publisher Services